Thankyou

ACKNOWLEDGEMENTS

To my husband BILL - I am so grateful for everything you have done to help make this book a reality. Thank you for your unconditional love and support.

To my daughters KELLIE, RACHEL & JENNA –Your encouraging words are what keep me going, I am so proud of you girls and love you very much.

To my sister LINDA – Thank you for your valuable thoughts and ideas, and for creating the title 'SYMPLY TOO GOOD TO BE TRUE'.

To my manager BEBE – Your belief in me is second to none. You are not only a fantastic manager but also a good friend and I look forward to what's ahead for the both of us. Ph: Bebe (07) 3630 4332.

To my tour manager STUART – Thankyou for organising my tours so well. Touring can be hard work but you make it easier and more enjoyable.

To my photographer SALLY – I am continually amazed by your talent, patience and ability to know just what I want. You really are a treasure. Ph: Sally (07) 5474 9129.

To my food stylist BILL – You once again have shown your incredible talent with food. Your patience and guidance was greatly appreciated.

To DIETITIANS – Effie Houvardas & Melinda Morrison from DIABETES AUSTRALIA-NSW – Your advice and guidance has been greatly appreciated. I hope through our association many people will benefit. Phone Diabetes Australia for any enquiries ring toll free: 1800 640862.

To my printer – THE INK SPOT, Maroochydore –You have been with me from the beginning, now 4 years later, 2 more books and over 600,000 copies printed you are still No. 1 to me. Thanks John, Christine, Ian and team for another job well done. Ph: (07) 5443 5431.

Artwork & colour separations GRAPHIC SKILLS, Maroochydore – To Steve, Naomi and crew, your expertise has once again produced an exceptional book. Ph: (07) 5479 1833.

To MYERS, Maroochydore – I had so much fun choosing from the vast array of beautiful crockery and kitchen wear for the photos. Thank you Glenda, Rashelle, Glen & Dot for your assistance.

To my distributors NETWORK DISTRIBUTION COMPANY – A big thankyou to Debbie, Sherryl, Margaret, Ainslee, Michael & Anton. You have all helped me to achieve what some would say was impossible. Phone: (07) 3865 1640.

To CORPORATE CORDS –Thank you for bringing out the best in me. Ph: Gretal (07) 3374 2522.

My store promotion assistances TREVOR, JEANETTE & KATH –Your ever-smiling faces, willingness to do whatever is needed and enthusiasm has helped me more than you could ever know.

My proof readers FIONA, BEBE, STUART, SUE & LEETA - I appreciate the time and effort you all put in to doing such a fantastic job. A special thank you to precious Fiona.

To my FAMILY and FRIENDS – who have always supported me in the good and bad times but have also proved to be skilled taste testers. Thank you to Jan, George, Kim, Shirley, Bill, Vicki, Dirk, Trevor, Jeanette and Paul. I am blessed to have such wonderful people who only bring sunshine into my life. A special thank you to my Mum, who is so proud, and supports me beyond anything, I love you Mum.

And finally I would like to thank every person who has one of my cookbooks. Through word of mouth I have achieved more than I could have ever hoped for. I wrote my books to help as many people as I could to better their lives. But in the process I have been given back more than anyone could dream of.

Thank you everyone from the bottom of my healthy heart!

MW00343822

Blueberry Flapjacks, page 13

Welcome Back Again. . .

Welcome back again to my world of tasty low fat cooking! They say three times lucky, so here is SYMPLY TOO GOOD TO BE TRUE '3'. Thank you to all the people who pushed me into writing this book - I wasn't sure I had another book in me, but after playing with a few recipes I was quickly on a roll with recipes coming out of me thick and fast, like a woman possessed. In the past there were a lot of fabulous recipes I believed were impossible to convert to low fat without losing their flavour. Then I thought, "Come on Annette if anyone can do it, you can," so began Book 3. I am so excited and when you see how I have transformed recipes that would normally be a no-no, you're just going to love this book and even better, they are now 'GUILT FREE'.

So what's new in this book? Completely different recipes from my other 2 books – no recipes are repeated. I have created 2 new sections – BREAKFASTS and SAUCES FOR PASTA. These sections were added due to so many people asking for them.

The nutritional inclusion of SATURATED FATS and SODIUM, will be of great value to anyone concerned with diabetes, heart or cholesterol problems. Diabetes is at plague proportions in Australia and New Zealand and as my recipes are suitable for diabetics and recommended by most health associations, I thought it also important to include relevant information on diabetes - I have included 2 pages of information written by dietitians Melinda Morrison and Effie Houvardas from DIABETES AUSTRALIA – NSW, who have also written the DIETITIAN'S TIPS.

And yes, there are more motivating testimonials - and then there are the recipes… they really are *simply too good to be true!*

If you are wanting to lose some weight, or have diabetes, heart or cholesterol problems, or just like to eat healthy food, then this book is recommended for you all; enjoy – guilt free at last.

I cannot believe the success of my books - with sales now exceeding half a million and sold internationally too. I never dreamt this would happen way back in November 1997 when I launched my first cookbook. Thank you to my faithful readers, with all my heart, for supporting me. I couldn't have done it without your help. Thank you for spreading the word. I hope that my new cookbook, SYMPLY TOO GOOD TO BE TRUE '3', will give you enjoyment and will be of value to you.

ENJOY EVERY MOUTHFUL!

ANNETTE'S STORY

As I reflect back over my life, memories as a chubby child, cuddly teenager, buxom bride and an obese adult come to mind. This is a story of how I was able to turn my greatest weakness into my greatest strength - having once weighed 100 kilos and successfully losing 35 kilos, I have maintained this weight for over 7 years. My journey has been filled with many highs and lows, battling years of obesity. Lets go back to where it all began…..

A Chubby Child...

Being the fattest kid in my class was something that I got used too. Everyone told me (and my mum) that it was 'puppy fat' and I would lose it, so I lived in ignorant bliss and just waited for the day that it would all melt away. That day never came. Life continued where I had to buy my clothes from the women's section, as the children's section could not accommodate my size. Being overweight as a kid wasn't easy, so I made up for it by being happy and outgoing, all the time desperate to fit in, yet crying on the inside. My way of surviving was to laugh at myself and dream of the day that I would look like all the other girls; I just wanted to be normal.

Cuddly Teenager...

Into puberty, I finally gave up on the hope of the 'puppy fat' miraculously going. At 13 I weighed 83 kilos and discovered dieting. This is where it all started - at such a young age I began what would be a lifetime of one diet after another. A doctor gave me diet pills and boy did I lose weight! When I think back I am horrified at what my eating pattern was like - I would eat nothing until lunchtime and then lunch was only an apple or a yoghurt. Dinner was a piece of steak, a little mashed potato and peas. Yes, the weight did fall off me but as you would expect, I couldn't sustain this restricted diet and too soon I was back eating the wrong foods and the weight came back with a vengeance. Teenagers can be so cruel, and nicknames cut deep; mine was "porky".

Buxom Bride...

I was married at 19 to the man of my dreams. I had to have my wedding dress made as I weighed around 80 kilos at the time and if you were over size 16 you had to get your clothes made for you. It was a lovely dress but not what I would have picked if I had been a size 12. Bill and I have now been married some 27 years and he truly is the most incredible person I have ever met. His love for me is unconditional. He never cared what size I was and hasn't ever suggested that I should go on a diet. After two years of contented, blissful marriage my weight blew up to 95 kilos. I really was getting fatter by the minute. I remember one time I was in a shop and the man behind the counter asked me when was I "due". I mumbled some sort of response and just ran home sobbing my fat little heart out. The funny thing is that you would think that would make me lose weight, but all it did was turn me more to my old friend food for comfort.

Obese Adult...

This is where my true addiction to food really took over. Food was my best friend, it didn't judge me and was always there for me. I was always on some sort of diet, searching for the easy way to lose weight. There were crazy diets that involved starving, liquid only diets, pills, hypnosis, pre-packaged meals, every diet book and magazines that I could find, and lets not forget the cabbage soup diet – that was a real doozy! All these diets achieved was weight gain and money wasted. Having three children only made the battle harder, but occasionally I did have successes. Looking through my photo albums, some years were not too bad, but eventually I would re-gain my weight and more. One day I had a life changing experience when my best friend Kim took a photo of me at Mooloolaba beach (January 1992). I weighed 100 kilos and was feeling very self-conscious. Two weeks later she sent me the photo. It was like a slap across the face. I cried the whole day; I had reached as low as I could go. As I wiped away the tears, something happened - I stopped feeling sorry for myself and decided that I had to do something about it. I stopped dieting and the rest is history; I not only conquered my weight problem but also created a life filled with an abundance of happiness. I turned my greatest weakness into my greatest strength.

Healthy Person...

The old Annette at 100 kilos,
The healthy Annette at 65 kilos.

The day I stopped dieting is the day I won the battle of the bulge. Learning to cook my favourite meals the low fat way, getting active and embracing the concept of 'being a healthy person' changed my life and I know if you can relate to my story then you too can change your life. My story is about being addicted to food and turning my life around to become a person who is now healthy and eating delicious food. My story is about daring to dream, embracing that dream and running with it. Don't wait another minute, empower yourself to be the best you can be and believe that it will happen. Don't let anything stand in your way and don't believe for another moment that you don't deserve to wear the clothes you want to, to feel good about yourself and to love yourself. Don't wait for a slap across the face situation like I did. Start now and change your life. All it takes is for you to make the decision like I did, become a healthy person and reap the rewards. Be your own best friend, not your worst enemy. Talk to yourself in a loving way and forget all the past failures. Start with a fresh, new attitude and remember, if I did it, so can you!

Diabetes and Good Nutrition – It's Symple!

Symply Too Good To Be True! Annette has put together another wonderful collection of recipes which are great tasting and great for your health. Annette has a passion for cooking and she combines this with an understanding of the importance of good nutrition. Since the launch of Annette's cookbooks, she has had many calls from readers with diabetes who are interested in healthy eating. As dietitians working at Diabetes Australia NSW, we are constantly asked about recipes that are suitable for people with diabetes. We are happy to say that all of the Symply Too Good To Be True books provide sensible, no fuss recipes that are suitable for everyone including people with diabetes, those trying to lose weight and anyone interested in good health.

ALL ABOUT DIABETES

Diabetes is reaching epidemic proportions worldwide. In fact, recent research in Australia has shown that 1 in 4 adults has either diabetes or a condition of impaired glucose metabolism (this condition is associated with an increased risk of diabetes and heart disease).

WHAT IS DIABETES?

Diabetes is a condition where there is too much glucose (sugar) in the blood. This occurs because insulin (a hormone that helps control blood glucose levels) is either not being produced by the body's pancreas or is not able to work properly. Without insulin doing its job, glucose builds up in the blood leading to high blood glucose levels. Over time, this can cause serious health problems if not managed appropriately. There are two main types of diabetes:

TYPE 1

This type of diabetes occurs when the pancreas stops producing insulin. Although it can affect people of any age, it is usually diagnosed in children and young adults. Type 1 diabetes accounts for 10-15% of all cases, there is currently no cure and treatment is a healthy lifestyle combined with insulin injections for life.

TYPE 2

This type of diabetes is the most common, accounting for 85-90 of all cases. In Type 2 diabetes the pancreas still produces so insulin, however the body does not use it properly. This leads high blood glucose levels. Type 2 diabetes is managed by combination of a healthy diet, regular physical activity and in so cases, diabetes medication/insulin.

Many people with type 2 diabetes remain undiagnosed for seve years. In Australia it is estimated that half of the people w diabetes don't even know they have it! Common symptoms inclu feeling tired, increased thirst, passing urine more often, blurr vision and infections that don't heal.

TYPE 2 DIABETES: ARE YOU AT RISK?

The risk of diabetes increases with age but if you can identify w any of the following risk factors then you should see your doc for a check up (this must include a blood test for glucose a cholesterol):

- ✔ You have high blood pressure
- ✔ You are overweight
- ✔ You have a family history of diabetes
- ✔ You have heart disease or have had a heart attack
- ✔ You have/had high blood sugar levels during pregnancy (Gestational diabetes)
- ✔ You have recorded a borderline blood sugar level
- ✔ You have polycystic ovary syndrome and are overweight
- ✔ You are over 65
- ✔ You are an Aboriginal or Torres Strait Islander
- ✔ You are from the Pacific Islands, Indian sub-continent or Chinese cultural background

REDUCING YOUR RISK

By eating well, maintaining a healthy weight and keeping acti you can reduce your risk of Type 2 diabetes and heart disease. T Dietary Guidelines for Australians provide the basis for healt eating. They are:

1. Enjoy a wide variety of nutritious foods

2. Eat plenty of breads and cereals (preferably wholegrain), vegetables (including legumes) and fruits.

3. Eat a diet low in fat and, in particular, low in saturated fat.

4. Maintain a healthy body weight by balancing physical activity and food intake.

5. If you drink alcohol, limit your intake.

6. Eat only a moderate amount of sugars and foods containing added sugars

7. Choose low salt foods and use salt sparingly.

8. Eat foods containing calcium. This is particularly important for girls and women.

9. Eat foods containing iron. This applies particularly to girls, women, vegetarians and athletes.

Remember that healthy eating is just one side of the story. Regular physical activity is just as important for good health, so get moving!

HEALTHY EATING FOR PEOPLE WITH DIABETES

There is no such thing as a diet for diabetes. Healthy eating for people with diabetes is the same as healthy eating for everyone. There is no need to prepare separate meals or buy special foods, so relax and enjoy a nutritious diet!

In addition to following the Dietary Guidelines for Australians, there are a few extra considerations for people with diabetes. To help manage your diabetes:

Eat regular meals and snacks spread evenly over the day

This provides your body with a regular supply of energy and can help to control blood glucose levels.

Choose foods lower in fat and in particular low in saturated fats

Eating too much saturated fat can lead to weight gain, poor diabetes control and high blood cholesterol levels. Saturated fat is found mainly in animal foods, like meat, cheese, butter and full cream milk as well as in takeaway and many pre-packaged foods. All the recipes in Symply Too Good To Be True are low in saturated fat.

Include small amounts of the healthier fats

Some fat is important for good health. Use a variety of polyunsaturated and monounsaturated types to achieve a good balance. Healthier fats include poly and monounsaturated margarines and oils such as canola or olive, fish, avocado, nuts and seeds.

Include carbohydrate foods in your meals and snacks

Carbohydrate foods are the best source of energy for your body. They include breads and cereals, pasta, rice, starchy vegetables, fruit, legumes and some dairy products. The type as well as the amount of carbohydrate eaten at a meal is important for people with diabetes. Look for the dietitian's tips on serve size throughout the book.

All carbohydrate foods are digested to produce glucose but they do so at different rates - some slow, some fast. This is called the Glycaemic Index (GI). Foods with a low GI raise blood glucose more slowly than foods with a high GI. People with diabetes can benefit from including at least three low GI foods throughout the day, ideally one at each meal.

A myth that continues to surround diabetes is that the diet must be sugar free. We now know that this is not the case as the GI has shown that some types of sugar such as those found in fruit or milk convert to glucose more slowly in the body. While it is still important to limit foods which are concentrated sources of sugar (eg soft drinks, lollies and syrups) small amounts of sugar can be included as part of a lower fat, high fibre meal.

A word about salt

Many people with diabetes have high blood pressure and need to watch how much salt is in their diet. Well done Annette for including the sodium contents in this book. Some of the recipes may be a little high in salt so where possible choose salt reduced or no added salt ingredients.

SYMPLY GREAT FOR PEOPLE WITH DIABETES

Annette has created a variety of recipes that are low in fat but high in taste! The recipes in Symply Too Good To Be True are suitable for people with diabetes. All of the recipes include information about key nutrients such as total and saturated fat, fibre and carbohydrate. Look for our 'dietitians tips' throughout the book. We hope you and your family enjoy Annette's recipes. They truly make healthy eating both easy and enjoyable!

Melinda Morrison and Effie Houvardas
DIETITIANS
Diabetes Australia - NSW

Dietitions Tip   *Look for these bars throughout the book for our tips and advice to assist diabetics.*

Diabetes Australia are happy to assist you with any questions or concerns you may have. Ring on their toll free number 1800 640 862.

DIABETES AUSTRALIA
New South Wales

Annette's Tips

WANT TO LOSE SOME WEIGHT? HERE ARE 10 WAYS TO GET STARTED:-

1. Have realistic expectations - Losing ½ to 1 kilo a week is fantastic; any more and you could lose valuable muscle tone. Your excess weight didn't happen overnight so don't expect it to be gone overnight. Slow and steady is the way to go, lose too quickly and your weight may come back quickly;

2. Eat breakfast every day. This is the most important meal of the day as it kick-starts your metabolism. Missing breakfast can result in bad choices later in the day and cause bingeing;

3. Focus on becoming a healthy person. Don't obsess about weighing yourself too often (once a week is more than enough). Don't be a dieter; instead embrace good health and make lifestyle changes that will last forever. Change the habits which have held you back in the past. Change does take time, but if you never give up, you will get where you want to go eventually;

4. Read food labels. Spend time shopping and learn which fats and how many kilojoules are in the food you buy. Look for the word "diet" on labels. This means the product is both low in fat and low in sugar - perfect for anyone wanting to lose weight. Watch the serving suggestions and how much sugar is in the product as well;

5. To lose weight have around 25-30 grams of fat per day for women, 35-40 grams for men. If inactive, 20-25 grams per day for women or 30-35 grams for men. This is only a rough guide as everyone has a different ability to burn fat;

6. Exercise. The importance of exercise is that it is essential for well-being. It also increases the metabolism and is great for the whole body. I would suggest exercising 4-5 times a week. Don't exercise just to lose weight, but more for general well being. Your body was designed to move, so get off the couch and get active;

7. Stop feeling deprived. By converting your favourite meals into low fat versions, you will avoid boredom and the feeling of deprivation. If you enjoy a piece of cake, then make my recipes. Forget the high fat versions; this way you can "have your cake guilt free and eat it too." Train your taste buds to enjoy low fat foods. Prepared the right way you really won't know the difference;

8. Forget dieting. If you want to lose weight and keep it off forever then forget dieting! All dieting will achieve is yoyo-ing you to obesity and serious health problems;

9. Don't sabotage yourself. Instead help yourself achieve your goal. Take responsibility for yourself and do whatever it takes to be the healthy person you deserve to be; and

10. Be your own best friend. Stop feeling sorry for yourself; instead be your own best buddy. You know what you have to do, so just do it!

HERE ARE MY 12 TOP TIPS TO A HEALTHY LIFESTYLE:-

1. Read the labels on products. "Light" doesn't always mean low fat. For example Light Olive Oil only means it is light in colour or flavour. Light could also mean that it is light in quantity, salt, sugar, fat or texture. Look for products that are both low in fat and sugar. Cholesterol free means the product is low in saturated fats, but could still be a high fat product as they use vegetable oil instead of animal fat - ideal for someone watching his or her cholesterol but not so good for a slimmer;

2. Go for reduced fat dairy products. Give up full cream milk at nearly 10gms of fat per glass compared to skim milk at 0.2gms of fat. Avoid using cream; instead go to my recipe for Symple Cream or use evaporated light milk instead;

3. Always eat breakfast as it kicks-starts your metabolism for the day;

4. Drink at least 2 litres of water every day; dehydration can be mistaken for hunger and drinking adequate amounts of water really helps the body deal with fluid retention and getting rid of waste products;

5. Cut down on caffeine; I suggest you convert to de-caffeinated versions instead;

6. Junk food can consist of high fat, high sugar and high salt with very little fibre - best eaten occasionally;

7. Have alcohol in moderation; too much and healthy eating goes out the window. Alcohol is high in sugar, and if consumed too often, can cause weight gain;

8. Eat the quantities of food that your body needs. When serving your meal, always use the sizing guide of one third protein, one third carbohydrates and one third vegetables or salad. Think about how much your body needs, not what you want. You can never eat too many vegetables or salad but too many carbohydrates or proteins can cause weight gain. Everything in moderation is the key to portion sizing;

9. Take control of food. Do not allow food to control you;

10. A low sodium diet is beneficial as we are consuming far too much salt. By limiting the amount of salt in your diet, you can reduce fluid retention and also help lower blood pressure;

11. Exercise at least 4-5 times a week; and

12. Don't be a chronic dieter, instead come into my world and enjoy low fat food the way it should be. Be satisfied, full and not deprived. Be happy, think positive and live life to the fullest every day. I know you can do it!

10 TIPS TO LOW FAT COOKING:-

1. Use cooking sprays instead of adding oil or fats to the pan;

2. Buy lean meats, for example premium mince compared to hamburger mince. With hamburger mince the butcher just puts more fat in;

3. Take the skin off the chicken or better still, buy skinless chicken;

4. Forget deep-frying; instead grill, BBQ or bake using cooking spray;

5. Coconut cream the Symple way – evaporated light milk and a little imitation coconut essence;

6. Use low fat mayonnaises and no-oil dressings on your salads;

7. Choose only reduced fat margarines and milks;

8. Don't use the egg yolks when baking. The yolk has 6gms of fat and high in saturated fats. The egg white has all the nutrients and raising ability but no fat, so why put yolks in if they don't benefit the dish;

9. Adding bi-carb soda will make lighter cakes or muffins; and

10. Use apple sauce (in jar) instead of oil or butter in cakes/muffins. Apple sauce gives the moisture butter would normally give - but there is no fat in apples.

SYMPLE COOKING HINTS:-

● Most of the recipes in this book are suitable to be frozen.

● The apple sauce used in many of the baking recipes is like the apple sauce you'd put on your roast pork, readily available near the mustard section in supermarkets. If you make the apple sauce yourself, you must make it a very runny consistency.

● The left over egg yolks can be used to make a FACE MASK by combining a mashed banana, a few ground almonds with an egg yolk.

● To reduce sodium (salt) in the recipes omit the salt and use salt reduced products eg. salt reduced soy sauce, etc.

ARE YOU AN EMOTIONAL EATER?

Emotional eating can cause or create havoc with your weight. A block of chocolate or creamy cheesecake seems to make you feel better if you are unhappy, worried or stressed (for a short while anyway) but therein lies the real issue. Yes, you feel good for a while but then what happens? As you wipe away the crumbs, you are faced with what you have done which can leave you feeling guilty, a failure and frustrated. Believe me, food is not the answer.

Food won't solve your problems - if anything, food will make them worse. No matter how bad the situation, food definitely doesn't make it better. Ask yourself, "What is my relationship with food?" Most slim people they will say that food is nourishment for their body, but for an overweight person, food becomes more of a love/hate relationship. Previously I thought food was my best friend, something I could always rely on. It was always there for me, never judged me and did make me feel good - well sometimes anyway. No wonder I was so overweight and could never lose the weight. If you relate to my story then here are 3 tips to help:-

1. Distract yourself. Instead of turning to food when bored, lonely and sad or unhappy, get busy, go for a walk, phone a friend, go shopping or fix your garden up. Boredom can be dangerous - don't eat just because there is nothing else to do. Being busy helps keep your mind off food.

2. Take control. Focus on being healthy instead of being on a diet. Diets only make you fat and frustrated. Look at changing your relationship with food and empower yourself to take control of your eating habits. When in doubt say to yourself, "What would a healthy person do right now?" then do it.

3. Like yourself, and don't be too hard on yourself. When in doubt ask yourself what your best friend would tell you to do right now. Your attitude is the key to success. By loving yourself and changing bad habits you will create a lifestyle that you deserve. Be your own best friend, love yourself and know and value yourself.

The adjustable teaspoon & tablespoon etc can be purchased from my website www.symplytoogood.com.au or Ph: (07) 5493 6750

Measuring Cups and Spoons

In every recipe a metric measuring cup and spoons were used. For example the tablespoon I have used, equals 15 grams. If you were using a metal tablespoon be aware that it could measure from 20 to 30 grams a spoon. I didn't use a tea cup. When I say 1 cup of flour, I have used a 250ml measuring cup as shown.

Testimonials

Annette Sym,
POBox 833,
Buddina. Q. 4575

By reading your books I now understand how to eat properly. Being a long distance truck driver I like that there is no weighing, counting calories or adding points, it's so simple. I have gone from a size 122cm shorts to 107cm and 6XOS shirts to XXL. I am smaller now than when I got married 21 years ago. Thank you Annette for showing how to be satisfied and enjoy eating again. To this day I am still in disbelief that I have lost a total of 50 kilos and feel the best I have ever felt in my life.

John Moore - Pomona QLD

John before

John now, 50 kilos lighter

I bought both your books and I love them. My only problem is I can't seem to get through too many recipes because I cook something and then keep making the same thing. What I've cooked is yummy and the best part - easy and there is no problem finding the ingredients. Being able to freeze everything is a major bonus. I live alone so I find I'm only cooking twice a week - love that. I'm looking forward to number 3 but who knows how long before I tear myself away from the first 2. I just wanted to thank you for taking the hassle out of healthy cooking. I don't even think about anything, I cook it, I eat it and I'm not concerned about whether it's okay or not. Thanks for everything, and by the way I love the stinky bread.

Irene Loukas - East St Kilda VIC

12 months after having my 1st child I was still 15kg overweight and my self-esteem was at an all time low. I needed some low fat recipe books that were quick, easy and tasty - things my husband would eat! Your recipe books were the answer! I lost 15kg in 20 weeks and never felt better. I have now had my 2nd child and it took 3 weeks to get back to my pre-pregnancy weight. Thank you for giving us so many healthy, low fat alternatives!

Kylie Morgan - West Dapto NSW

My 8 year old daughter Lisa recently entered your recipe for WICKED CHOCOLATE CAKE at the Royal Easter Show. She entered in the children and student section for chocolate cakes and guess what?! She won first prize!!!

The judges had no idea the cake was low fat. We are all very proud of her achievement and thank you for such a delicious and easy recipe.

Ingrid Player - North Ryde NSW

The recipes and tips in your books and website combined with support from Croydon TOWN Club have helped me to lose 30kg (size 22 down to size 14) in 18 months. The pinnacle of my personal success came when I reached my goal weight and achieved "Graduate" status within the Club. The website is great with common sense tips to everyday "fat" problems. It has an "ongoing" feel, which backs up what you say in your books. Thank you for helping me take control of my life!

Christine Young - Croydon VIC

As my cholesterol had climbed to 6.0 I looked around for a fat free cookbook and was directed to yours. In 4 months my cholesterol has dropped to 4.3. It was never my real intention to lose weight, however much to my astonishment I lost 12 kilos! Your way of eating combined with a brisk 45 minute walk, 5 times a week, has satisfied my doctor with my weight, cholesterol and blood pressure readings. My doctor was so impressed he recommends your books to his patients. I owe you Annette. I am a 62 year old male, who has never felt better.

Don Budge - Salisbury QLD

I am writing to you, after reading your letter to my (34 year old) daughter, Re: her struggle with weight. What a lovely lady you must be to do that. I had no idea Leigh had written to you and even better, I had no idea famous people wrote back to people (like us). Keep up the good work and you must be doing a great job, if you made a difference in one person's life (my beautiful daughter's). Many thanks.

Sandra-Joy Robertson - Beerwah QLD

By following your philosophy on living, using your cookbooks and being inspired by your speaking, I have lost 18 kg and am feeling like living again. Running a business restricts my time greatly. I find your recipes quick and simple, making it easy to maintain good health.

Paula Jardine - Minyama QLD

My son Craig didn't exercise and lived on fast foods. His weight slowly escalated to 145 kg and as his father died of a heart attack at 55, I decided to help him lose the weight pronto!! I borrowed your 2 cookbooks and am most impressed with your recipes. It was very hard convincing my son that he can get away with some of your "Wicked Chocolate Cake" and still lose weight but seeing is believing. It is amazing with this change in lifestyle, your cookbooks and the support of Warwick Day Weight Reduction Club of Qld, he lost 33 kilos and 12 cm off his waist. What a relief not to worry about his health anymore, as he is now his old, trim self again.

Daphne Tange - Warwick QLD

Lindsay and I felt we needed to write and let you know how grateful we are that we have discovered your wonderful cookbooks.
My husband Lindsay lost 25 kilos in just 16 months and has kept it off, just by symply (excuse the pun) following your wonderful recipes which haven't left him feeling hungry or deprived of yummy food because it is all there in your books. But best of all, the whole family are eating the meals. Also, Lindsay found it easy to lose weight and didn't have to starve himself. He just had to be aware of what he was eating, do a little exercise and follow your delicious recipes, and presto he found the kilos coming off just like that. What we have found most of all is that we are not on a diet. We have just chosen a healthier way to eat in our lifestyle and with a little determination it has all been achievable thanks to you and your lovely cookbooks.

Lindsay & Jenny Heperi - Christchurch NEW ZEALAND

What a difference your cookbooks have made to my life. I now enjoy my food and only cook the low fat way. My family enjoys all the recipes and this means I don't have to cook different meals for the whole family. Both your books are the basis of my cooking, kind of like my cooking bible. After 12 months I had lost a total of 45 kg. I now go to the gym, do aerobics and still have energy for my family. The smile has returned, I am a lot happier in myself and enjoy my life now. My confidence has improved as my weight dropped and I now believe I can do whatever I put my mind too. I can't tell you how much your cookbooks have helped me, not only in losing my weight, but keeping it off for over 3 years.

Bronwyn Platt - Petrie QLD

As a working mother of 3 young children, I was inspired by your low fat recipe book that includes family size meals that are not only tasty but even my children like to eat. My husband has had high blood pressure for the last 10 years and has never been able to stick to a diet. He loves the meals and takes any leftovers (if any) to work for lunch the next day. We both added a daily walk and no fat milk to our lifestyle and the results are amazing. In only 9 weeks we both lost 8 kilos and feel great. Our friends keep asking how we did it and I say it is *"Simply Too Good To Be True"*. As a nurse I know the importance of a healthy diet and I never thought it could be so easy.

Bernadette Smith - Ferny Grove QLD

My wife bought me your cookbooks after I was diagnosed with type 2 diabetes. Since then, I have lost (and kept off) 16 kg, and my diabetes is under control without drugs. Annette's 'symple', common-sense dietary advice, tasty recipes and cooking tips have made a huge contribution to my success.

Robin Shaw - Adelaide SA

I recently ordered your two recipe books from your web site and I just wanted to say thank you!! The meals are all so delicious, but most importantly they are quick and easy! Being a brand new wife, it's been tough coming home from a hard day's work to prepare a healthy meal, but now with your recipes I can't wait to get home and start cooking. What a great idea to include kilojoules and fat grams for each recipe. I've teamed your recipes with Weight Watchers and with your nutritional information, I can easily work out how many points each serving is.

Vanessa Nuzzo - Caroline Springs VIC

I am writing to thank you. I injured my back in October 1999 and managed to gain 21 kg. After a very long recovery process I decided to lose some weight. My mother told me about your books and after some scepticism I decided to try out your recipes. By following your recipes I have managed to lose 16 kilos and am in better shape now than before my back injury.

Matt - South Perth WA

Thank you for your inspirational talk at Diabetes Auckland. I was very highly motivated and bought your 2 books and have used many recipes. Consequently I have managed to lose 18 kilos to the delight of my specialist.

Robyn James - Auckland NEW ZEALAND

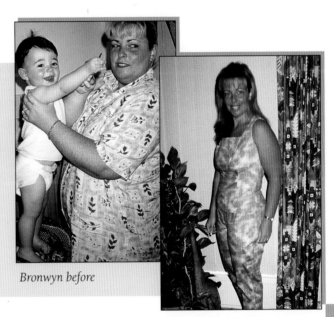
Bronwyn before

Bronwyn now, 45 kilos lighter

Your books are the most aptly named I have struck. Since our introduction to them we have taken on a whole new lease of life. Seven months ago I started using your recipes and advice given almost exclusively, and adapted old favourites, using the low fat products as recommended by you. After 3-4 months - quite a shock to discover I had a significant weight loss. It was so easy I hadn't realised it was happening, I have now lost 15 kg to date. Thank you for changing and improving our lifestyle.

June Hayden - Whangarei NEW ZEALAND

Many thanks for your wonderful cookbooks. On April 11th this year my husband had a stroke and a cholesterol reading of 7.4. The dietitian from the Sunshine Hospital viewed your books 1 & 2 and said that, if we kept to your recipes, we couldn't go wrong. She was going to purchase a set for the hospital. My husband has progressed really well and his cholesterol level is down to 3.7. Great Books!

Marg & Bill O'Connell - Sunshine VIC

BIG BREAKFAST

SERVES: 1

1 egg
2-3 slices (50g) lean short cut bacon
1 tomato sliced in half
1-2 large mushrooms sliced
$^1/_3$ cup baked beans
cooking spray

In a non-stick frypan generously coated with cooking spray fry egg, bacon, mushrooms and tomato. Heat baked beans in microwave.

Dietitions Tip *What a winner, a hearty breakfast that is much lower in fat than the traditional version.*

NUTRITIONAL INFORMATION

PER SERVE			PER SERVE	
FAT	TOTAL	8.3g	CARBOHYDRATES	13.2g
	SATURATED	2.6g	SODIUM	1182mg
FIBRE		6.4g	KILOJOULES	922 (cal 220)
PROTEIN		23.0g		

FRENCH TOAST

SERVES: 2

4 slices toast bread
2 egg whites
$^1/_3$ cup skim milk
2 tablespoons sugar
dash vanilla essence
$^1/_2$ teaspoon cinnamon
cooking spray

In a medium size mixing bowl beat all ingredients together except the bread. Dip one bread slice at a time in milk mixture until coated. Place each slice into a heated non-stick frypan, (not on full temperature or it will burn) that has been coated with cooking spray and fry for about 5 minutes or until browned then turn and cook a further 5 minutes or until browned.

Dietitions Tip
A great alternative to traditional French toast.

NUTRITIONAL INFORMATION:

PER SERVE		
FAT	TOTAL	0.9g
	SATURATED	0.2g
FIBRE		1.0g
PROTEIN		5.7g
CARBOHYDRATES		25.7g
SODIUM		213mg
KILOJOULES		555 (cal 132)

HAM & CHEESE OMELETTE

SERVES: 1

3 egg whites
$^1/_4$ cup grated 25% reduced fat tasty cheese
$^1/_4$ cup (20g) sliced ham
cooking spray

In a medium size mixing bowl beat egg whites until stiff peaks form. Using a knife gently fold in cheese and ham. In a heated non-stick frypan coated with cooking spray pour mixture into centre. Cook for 3 minutes on moderate heat (the base will burn otherwise) until golden brown, turn gently and cook a further 3 minutes or until cooked.

VARIATION: Omit cheese and ham for a PLAIN OMELETTE

Dietitions Tip *A delicious omelette.*
To reduce salt try substituting the ham for $^1/_2$ cup chopped capsicum and mushrooms.

NUTRITIONAL INFORMATION:

PER SERVE		H/CHEESE	PLAIN
FAT	TOTAL	5.5g	0g
	SATURATED	3.3g	0g
FIBRE		0g	0g
PROTEIN		20.0g	10.4g
CARBOHYDRATES		0.4g	0.4g
SODIUM		623mg	163mg
KILOJOULES		548 (cal 130)	183 (cal 44)

CREAMY KIDNEYS

SERVES: 2

250g lamb kidneys
1 Lite Mushroom & Chive Cup-A-Soup® sachet
3/4 cup evaporated light milk
1 tablespoon finely chopped parsley
2 teaspoons corn flour
cooking spray

Remove sinew from middle of each kidney then dice. In a non-stick saucepan that has been coated with cooking spray sauté kidneys until cooked. In a small mixing bowl add milk, soup mix, parsley and corn flour, blend with a fork, add to saucepan, bring to boil stirring continuously.

Dietitions Tip *If you have high blood cholesterol levels, enjoy this dish occasionally.*

NUTRITIONAL INFORMATION:

PER SERVE		
FAT	TOTAL	5.5g
	SATURATED	2.6g
FIBRE		0.8g
PROTEIN		22.6g
CARBOHYDRATES		16.3g
SODIUM		722mg
KILOJOULES		976 (cal 233)

CORN FRITTERS

SERVES: 6

1 x 425g can creamed corn
1 cup corn kernels
1/4 cup onion finely diced
1/2 cup self raising flour
1 egg white
1/4 teaspoon dried basil
1 tablespoon chopped parsley
2 teaspoons chicken stock powder
cooking spray

In a large mixing bowl combine creamed corn, corn kernels, onion, stock powder, basil and parsley. In a small mixing bowl beat egg white for 30 seconds and add to corn mixture. Fold in flour until combined. In a non-stick frypan (at moderate hot temperature) coated with cooking spray place large spoonfuls of mixture into pan, spread each fritter into a round shape. Cook 5 minutes or until browned, then turn, press down with spatula and cook a further 5 minutes. Makes 12 fritters.

NUTRITIONAL INFORMATION:

PER SERVE			PER SERVE	
FAT	TOTAL	1.1g	CARBOHYDRATES	45.0g
	SATURATED	0.2g	SODIUM	696mg
FIBRE		10.3g	KILOJOULES	996 (cal 131)
PROTEIN		11.2g		

TOFU SCRAMBLE

SERVES: 4

375g firm tofu
1/4 cup onion finely chopped
2 tablespoons chopped parsley
1 teaspoon vegetable stock powder
salt and pepper to taste
4 slices white bread (toasted)
cooking spray

Drain liquid from tofu and place in a medium size mixing bowl, mash tofu using a potato masher. In a non-stick frypan that has been coated with cooking spray sauté onion for 2 minutes. Reduce heat to medium and add in tofu, parsley and stock powder, cook 1 minute then season to taste. Serve over toast.

NUTRITIONAL INFORMATION:

PER SERVE			PER SERVE	
FAT	TOTAL	6.4g	CARBOHYDRATES	18.0g
	SATURATED	0.2g	SODIUM	375mg
FIBRE		1.0g	KILOJOULES	646 (cal 154)
PROTEIN		12.1g		

BLUEBERRY FLAPJACKS

SERVES: 6

BATTER
1 x 425g can blueberries
1 cup self raising flour
2 egg whites
¹/₄ cup sugar
¹/₂ cup skim milk
¹/₄ teaspoon vanilla essence
³/₄ teaspoon bi-carb soda
cooking spray

SAUCE
saved juice from canned blueberries
1 tablespoon corn flour

BATTER Drain blueberries, save juice from can to make sauce. In a medium size mixing bowl beat egg whites and sugar for 1 minute. Mix in essence and milk. Sift flour and bi-carb into mixture in one go, DO NOT BEAT but gently fold flour through until just combined (over beating bruises the flour and will make the flapjacks tough). Fold blueberries through the dough gently. Coat a non-stick frypan with cooking spray and pour a little less than half a cup (100mls) of mixture into pan, spread dough to make a round shape. Cook 1-2 minutes or until browned, turn and cook another minute or so until cooked. Repeat until all mixture has been used. Makes 6 flapjacks.

SAUCE In a small saucepan combine the saved juice and corn flour, stirring continuously. When boiled pour sauce over each flapjack.

VARIATIONS:
Replace blueberries with 2 cups FRESH APPLE peeled and finely diced.
Instead of sauce make CINNAMON SUGAR by mixing 4 teaspoons sugar and 1 teaspoon cinnamon together, sprinkle over flapjacks
or OMIT THE SAUCE - it will reduce carbohydrate count to 31.5g, kilojoules 612 (cal 146)

NUTRITIONAL INFORMATION:					
PER SERVE	B/BERRY	APPLE	PER SERVE	B/BERRY	APPLE
FAT TOTAL	0.4g	0.4g	CARBOHYDRATES	38.3g	33.0g
SATURATED	0.1g	0.1g	SODIUM	193mg	190mg
FIBRE	3.6g	1.0g	KILOJOULES	792 (cal 174)	635 (cals 151)
PROTEIN	4.8g	4.4g			

BANANA SMOOTHIE

MAKES: 1

1 medium size ripe banana (preferably cold)
6 cubes of ice
1 cup cold skim milk
1 teaspoon sugar (optional)
a few drops vanilla essence
a few drops coconut essence (optional)

Place ice cubes into a blender and crush. Place all other ingredients into blender and blend until thick. The colder the milk and banana the thicker the smoothie.

VARIATIONS:
Replace banana with PINEAPPLE, STRAW-BERRIES OR ANY FRUIT you desire,
or replace coconut essence with RUM ESSENCE.

NUTRITIONAL INFORMATION:			
PER SMOOTHIE		PER SMOOTHIE	
FAT TOTAL	0.4g	CARBOHYDRATES	40.3g
SATURATED	0.3g	SODIUM	115mg
FIBRE	2.6g	KILOJOULES	861 (cal 205)
PROTEIN	11.3g		

SPRING ROLLS

MAKES: 12

3/4 cup cooked lean pork mince
2 cups cabbage finely shredded
I cup celery cut into thin strips
I cup carrot cut into thin strips
1/2 cup shallots chopped
1/2 cup bamboo shoots cut into thin strips
3/4 cup Singapore noodles
12 spring roll wraps
2 teaspoons chicken stock powder
I teaspoon sugar
1/2 teaspoon crushed ginger (in jar)
1/2 teaspoon crushed garlic (in jar)
I teaspoon fish sauce
I teaspoon soy sauce
2 tablespoons oyster sauce
cooking spray

Preheat oven to 210°C fan forced.

In a large saucepan coated with cooking spray place all the ingredients except cooked mince, noodles and spring roll wraps. Once vegetables are cooked add mince and noodles and stir together. Gently peel off a spring roll wrap, place diagonally in front of you. On the point closest to you place about a third of a cup of the mixture. Either follow instructions on back of wrapper or, taking the point closest to you, fold over the filling then bring left and right sides over filling and roll away from yourself, making a spring roll shape. Place rolls on a flat baking tray coated with cooking spray and then give the tops a spray as well. Bake for 15-20 minutes or until browned.

> *Dietitions Tip*   Annette has done a great job with these low fat spring rolls. They are a little high in salt so people with diabetes may want to enjoy these in moderation.

NUTRITIONAL INFORMATION:

PER SERVE (I SPRING ROLL)

FAT	TOTAL	0.7g
	SATURATED	0.2g
FIBRE		1.6g
PROTEIN		5.0g
CARBOHYDRATES		16.3g
SODIUM		409mg
KILOJOULES		389 (cal 93)

CHICKEN BITES

SERVES: 6

500g chicken fillets
3/4 cup dried breadcrumbs
I egg white
1/4 cup skim milk
3/4 teaspoon dried basil
I teaspoon chicken stock powder
cooking spray

Preheat oven to 200°C fan forced.

On a large plate combine breadcrumbs, basil and stock powder. On another large plate beat the egg white and milk together. Cut chicken fillets in half then coat with milk mix, cover generously with breadcrumbs then place on a flat baking tray that has been coated with cooking spray. Coat the chicken pieces with cooking spray and bake for 10 minutes, turn chicken pieces over and spray again with cooking spray, bake a further 10 minutes. Don't over cook as they will become dry. Serve with sauce of your choice.

NUTRITIONAL INFORMATION:

PER SERVE

FAT	TOTAL	4.0g
	SATURATED	1.1g
FIBRE		0.4g
PROTEIN		19.8g
CARBOHYDRATES		8.1g
SODIUM		302mg
KILOJOULES		621 (cal 148)

HERB BREAD

MAKES: 15 Slices

3/4 teaspoon dried mixed herbs
1/2 tablespoon chopped parsley
2 tablespoons reduced fat margarine (Flora® light)
2 teaspoons skim milk
1 x 170g French bread stick

In a small mixing bowl beat margarine for one minute, slowly add in milk, about 1/2 teaspoon at a time until blended. Toss in herbs and parsley and combine well. Cut bread stick into 15 slices, spread margarine mix over the top of each slice and place under griller until golden brown.

Dietitions Tip *This is a winner, usually dripping in fat, Annette has revamped an old favourite everyone can enjoy!*

NUTRITIONAL INFORMATION:

PER SLICE		
FAT	TOTAL	1.3g
	SATURATED	0.3g
FIBRE		0.4g
PROTEIN		1.1g
CARBOHYDRATES		5.5g
SODIUM		87mg
KILOJOULES		160 (cal 38)

GARLIC BREAD

MAKES: 15 Slices

3 teaspoons crushed garlic (in jar)
1 tablespoon chopped parsley
2 tablespoons reduced fat margarine (Flora® light)
2 teaspoons skim milk
1 x 170g French bread stick

In a small mixing bowl beat margarine for one minute, slowly add in milk, about 1/2 teaspoon at a time until blended. Toss in garlic and parsley, combine well. Cut bread stick into 15 slices, spread margarine mix over the top of each slice and place under griller until golden brown.

Dietitions Tip *To increase the fibre in these recipes try using a high fibre white, wholemeal or grain bread.*

NUTRITIONAL INFORMATION:

PER SLICE		
FAT	TOTAL	1.3g
	SATURATED	0.3g
FIBRE		0.5g
PROTEIN		1.2g
CARBOHYDRATES		5.6g
SODIUM		87mg
KILOJOULES		163 (cal 39)

OYSTERS MORNAY

SERVES: 4

2 dozen shell oysters
1 ¹/₂ cups skim milk
1 tablespoon reduced fat margarine (Flora® light)
2 tablespoons plain flour
¹/₂ cup grated 25% reduced fat tasty cheese

In a small saucepan melt margarine, add flour and cook for 30 seconds. Slowly whisk in milk, stirring continuously to avoid lumps. Leave to cool slightly. Put oysters on a flat baking tray. Spoon white sauce over each oyster then sprinkle a little cheese over the top. Place oysters under a hot griller until cheese has melted and is golden brown.

Dietitians Tip *A great alternative to the traditional recipe, well done Annette!*

NUTRITIONAL INFORMATION:

PER SERVE

FAT	TOTAL	5.7g
	SATURATED	2.6g
FIBRE		0.2g
PROTEIN		11.3g
CARBOHYDRATES		9.2g
SODIUM		240mg
KILOJOULES		553 (cal 132)

OYSTERS KILPATRICK

SERVES: 4

2 dozen shell oysters
4 tablespoons BBQ sauce
6 teaspoons worcestershire sauce
190g lean short cut bacon

Trim excess fat off bacon, cut into small dice and combine with bbq and worcestershire sauce. Place oysters on a flat baking tray and spoon an even amount of mixture over top of each oyster. Place under a hot griller until bacon is cooked and crispy.

Dietitians Tip *This dish is high in salt, so people with diabetes enjoy this dish on special occasions.*

NUTRITIONAL INFORMATION:

PER SERVE

FAT	TOTAL	3.4g
	SATURATED	1.2g
FIBRE		0.3g
PROTEIN		14.0g
CARBOHYDRATES		14.0g
SODIUM		1099mg
KILOJOULES		590 (cal 141)

MEXICANA SOUP

SERVES: 10

1 x 420g can Mexican chilli beans

2 x 420g cans 4 bean mix (drained and rinsed)

1 x 425g can crushed tomatoes

1/2 cup red capsicum diced

1/2 cup green capsicum diced

1 cup onion diced

1 cup celery sliced

1 1/2 cups potato diced

1 x 35g pkt taco seasoning (Old El Paso®)

1 teaspoon crushed garlic (in jar)

1 teaspoon dried cumin

1 teaspoon dried coriander

2 teaspoons beef stock powder

10 cups water

cooking spray

In a boiler that has been coated with cooking spray sauté garlic, capsicum, onion, celery and potato for 2 minutes, add taco seasoning, beef stock powder, cumin and coriander and toss for 1 minute. Add all other remaining ingredients. Simmer for 60 minutes. Using a potato masher, mash ingredients in pot until a thick texture appears.

Dietitians Tip *A delicious and hearty soup packed with vegetables. Serve with toasted grain bread for a complete meal.*

NUTRITIONAL INFORMATION:

PER SERVE		
FAT	TOTAL	1.0g
	SATURATED	0.1g
FIBRE		9.3g
PROTEIN		9.0g
CARBOHYDRATES		26.0g
SODIUM		1073mg
KILOJOULES		630 (cal 150)

SYMPLE SOUR CREAM

SERVES: 10

1 x 500g tub low fat cottage cheese

2 tablespoons lemon juice

In a food processor beat cottage cheese until very smooth. Add lemon juice and combine well. Keep refrigerated.

NUTRITIONAL INFORMATION

PER SERVE		
FAT	TOTAL	0.6g
	SATURATED	0.4g
FIBRE		0g
PROTEIN		8.8g
CARBOHYDRATES		1.1g
SODIUM		65mg
KILOJOULES		192 (cal 46)

SWEET POTATO & CORN SOUP

SERVES: 8

1 kilo red sweet potato
1 x 420g can creamed corn
1 cup onion diced
1 teaspoon dried cumin
1 teaspoon crushed garlic (in jar)
2 tablespoons honey
4 teaspoons chicken stock powder
8 cups water
salt & pepper to taste
cooking spray

Peel and dice sweet potato. In a boiler that has been coated with cooking spray sauté garlic and onion for 1 minute. Add cumin, stock powder and sweet potato and toss together for 1 minute. Add water, honey and creamed corn, bring to boil, simmer 30 minutes. Puree in food processor or use a potato masher and mash until you get a smooth texture. Salt and pepper to taste.

> *Dietitions Tip* *Everyone will love this winter warmer! Sweet potato is a great choice for people with diabetes as it has a low GI.*

NUTRITIONAL INFORMATION:

PER SERVE		
FAT	TOTAL	0.8g
	SATURATED	0.2g
FIBRE		4.1g
PROTEIN		3.2g
CARBOHYDRATES		33.3g
SODIUM		638mg
KILOJOULES		637 (cal 152)

HEARTY VEGETABLE SOUP

SERVES: 10

2 cups carrot sliced
2 cups celery sliced
1 cup small florets broccoli
6 cups raw pumpkin small diced
1 cup onion diced
2 teaspoons crushed garlic (in jar)
3/4 cup dried soup mix (barley/split peas etc)
4 teaspoons vegetable stock powder
12 cups water
salt and pepper to taste
cooking spray

Chop up all vegetables. In a boiler that has been coated with cooking spray sauté onion and garlic for 1 minute. Add all other ingredients and simmer for 1 1/4 hours. Using a potato masher mash ingredients in pot until a thick consistency is achieved. Salt and pepper to taste.

> *Dietitions Tip* *Packed with vitamins and minerals, this soup is sure to please everyone!*

NUTRITIONAL INFORMATION:

PER SERVE		
FAT	TOTAL	0.9g
	SATURATED	0.4g
FIBRE		4.4g
PROTEIN		5.3g
CARBOHYDRATES		14.5g
SODIUM		405mg
KILOJOULES		370 (cal 88)

MEXICAN DIP

SERVES: 12 As an appetiser

1 x 450g can refried beans

1 x 300ml jar hot salsa (Masterfoods®)

$^1/_2$ cup (125g) avocado mashed

$^1/_4$ cup grated 25% reduced fat tasty cheese

1 tablespoon taco seasoning (Old El Paso®)

$^1/_2$ cup tomato diced

$^1/_4$ cup capsicum diced

2 shallots sliced

1 x 200g tub low fat natural yoghurt

In a medium size mixing bowl combine refried beans and jar of salsa together. Spread over base of a pie dish. Mix the taco seasoning with avocado and gently spread over top of bean mix. Spread yoghurt over avocado then sprinkle cheese, tomato, shallots and capsicum over top of yoghurt. Refrigerate until required. Serve with rice crackers or my corn chips (from book 1 on page 15).

VARIATION:
Replace yoghurt with half batch 'SYMPLE SOUR CREAM' page 18. Add 0.6 grams of fat per serve.

Dietitions Tip Kidney beans (refried) are low in fat, high in fibre and have a low GI.

NUTRITIONAL INFORMATION:		
PER SERVE		
FAT	TOTAL	3.5g
	SATURATED	1.0g
FIBRE		2.3g
PROTEIN		4.0g
CARBOHYDRATES		10.2g
SODIUM		427mg
KILOJOULES		360 (cal 86)

CHEESY SPINACH BREAD DIP

SERVES: 12 As an appetiser

1 x 475g cob loaf
1 pkt cheese and leek soup mix
1 tablespoon reduced fat margarine (Flora® light)
2 cups skim milk
1 heaped tablespoon plain flour
1/4 cup onion finely diced
1 x 250g pkt frozen chopped spinach

Preheat oven to 180°C fan forced.

Defrost spinach and leave to one side to drain. In a non-stick saucepan that has been coated with cooking spray sauté onion and margarine for 1 minute, add flour and combine. Add soup mix to milk and blend together. Using a whisk slowly add milk to saucepan stirring continuously until mixture boils. Stir in defrosted spinach and bring to boil, leave to one side until bread is ready.

Cut a hole in the top of the loaf, about the size of a small side plate. Pull out middle of bread in chunks and cut the centre piece into chunks. Place bread on a flat baking tray and bake for 10 minutes. Pour cheese sauce into loaf and serve with pieces of bread around the edge for dipping. Cheese sauce can be served hot or cold.

NUTRITIONAL INFORMATION:		
PER SERVE		
FAT	TOTAL	3.0g
	SATURATED	0.4g
FIBRE		2.3g
PROTEIN		7.3g
CARBOHYDRATES		27.2g
SODIUM		608mg
KILOJOULES		697 (cal 166)

HAM & CHEESE ROLLS

SERVES: 6

12 Sheets filo pastry
12 slices Devondale Seven® single cheese
6 shallots
180g lean ham
1 x 300ml jar mild salsa (Masterfoods®)
cooking spray

Preheat oven to 180°C fan forced.

Lay out one sheet of filo pastry and spray with cooking spray, cut sheet in half and place one on top of the other. In the middle of the edge closest to you place 1/2 of one cheese slice, on top of the cheese lay half a shallot stick then top with a twelfth of the ham. Finally top with the remaining half of the cheese slice. Fold right and left edges in, roll away from yourself rolling tightly. This should form a roll similar looking to a spring roll. Place rolls on a flat baking tray that has been coated with cooking spray, lightly coat rolls with spray, bake 15-20 minutes or until golden brown. Heat salsa and spoon over each roll.

NOTE: *I personally find the filo pastry that is not frozen (ANTONIOU®) is much easier to work with. You will find it in your supermarket refrigeration section.*

NUTRITIONAL INFORMATION:		
PER SERVE		(2 ROLLS)
FAT	TOTAL	4.8g
	SATURATED	3.5g
FIBRE		0.4g
PROTEIN		19.7g
CARBOHYDRATES		22.0g
SODIUM		1555mg
KILOJOULES		873 (cal 208)

GREEK SALAD

SERVES: 3 large or 6 as a side dish

1/2 cup red capsicum cubed

1/2 cup green capsicum cubed

I cup Spanish onion thinly sliced

1 1/2 cups continental cucumber cubed

1/2 cup celery sliced

I cup tomatoes cut in cubes

I cos lettuce

I cup reduced fat feta cheese cubed

1/2 cup sliced Spanish olives

1/3 cup no oil fat free French dressing (Kraft®)

I teaspoon crushed garlic (in jar)

I teaspoon French mustard

In a small container combine dressing, garlic and mustard, secure lid and shake well. Tear lettuce into pieces. In a large salad bowl place lettuce, tomato, capsicum, onion, cucumber and celery, toss together. Sprinkle the cheese, olives and dressing over salad and toss together.

NUTRITIONAL INFORMATION:		
PER SERVE	LARGE	S/DISH
FAT TOTAL	7.4g	3.7g
SATURATED	3.7g	1.6g
FIBRE	4.4g	2.2g
PROTEIN	16.2g	8.1g
CARBOHYDRATES	24.0g	12.0g
SODIUM	1180mg	590mg
KILOJOULES	684 (cal 163)	342 (cal 81)

ASIAN SALAD

SERVES: 10

I Chinese cabbage (wombok) shredded

1/2 cup shallots chopped

I cup Chang's® Fried Noodles

1/3 cup slivered almonds

1/2 cup celery sliced

2 tablespoons sesame seeds

1/2 cup no oil fat free French dressing (Kraft®)

I tablespoon soy sauce

1/3 cup brown sugar

On a griller tray covered with a sheet of alfoil, toast almonds until browned (be careful not to burn them) remove and leave to one side. Place sesame seeds under griller like almonds and brown, they brown very quickly so keep an eye on them. In a small container combine dressing, soy sauce and sugar, put lid on securely and shake until sugar has dissolved. Place shredded cabbage, sliced celery and shallots in a large serving bowl. When ready to serve toss the noodles, sesame seeds, almonds and dressing with cabbage at the last minute as the noodles soften quickly.

NUTRITIONAL INFORMATION:	
PER SERVE	
FAT TOTAL	4.5g
SATURATED	0.6g
FIBRE	2.4g
PROTEIN	3.2g
CARBOHYDRATES	9.0g
SODIUM	339mg
KILOJOULES	377 (cal 90)

23

BEETROOT IN SOUR CREAM

SERVES: 6 As a side dish

2 large (500g) fresh beetroots
1 shallot finely sliced
1/2 cup low fat cottage cheese
1 teaspoon lemon juice
salt and pepper to taste

Peel and dice beetroots. Microwave in a small amount of water for 10-12 minutes on high or until beetroot is soft, drain well and place in a medium size mixing bowl. In food processor blend cottage cheese until smooth, add lemon juice and mix well. Fold cheese mixture, shallots and beetroot together. Serve either hot or cold.

VARIATION: Replace cottage cheese with 1/2 cup NATURAL LIGHT YOGHURT, omit lemon juice.

NUTRITIONAL INFORMATION		
PER SERVE		
FAT	TOTAL	0.3g
	SATURATED	0.2g
FIBRE		2.6g
PROTEIN		5.3g
CARBOHYDRATES		7.4g
SODIUM		73mg
KILOJOULES		224 (cal 54)

CAULIFLOWER AU GRATIN

SERVES: 4 As a side dish

600g cauliflower
1 1/2 cups skim milk
1 tablespoon reduced fat margarine
(Flora® light)
2 tablespoons plain flour
1/3 cup grated 25% reduced fat tasty cheese
salt & pepper to taste

Boil or microwave cauliflower to your liking. While cauliflower is cooking melt margarine in a medium size saucepan, add flour and mix together. Gradually beat in milk (use a whisk to avoid lumps) until white sauce is made. Leave to one side for 5 minutes to allow sauce to thicken. Place cauliflower in a casserole dish and pour sauce over, sprinkle cheese on top. Place under griller until cheese is golden brown.

NUTRITIONAL INFORMATION:		
PER SERVE		
FAT	TOTAL	3.5g
	SATURATED	1.3g
FIBRE		1.6g
PROTEIN		7.0g
CARBOHYDRATES		7.6g
SODIUM		99mg
KILOJOULES		375 (cal 89)

HONEY CARROTS

SERVES: 6 As a side dish

3 cups (400g) carrots sliced
2 tablespoons honey
2 teaspoons reduced fat margarine (Flora® light)

Cook carrots in microwave to your liking. In a non-stick saucepan melt margarine, add honey and bring to boil. Toss in drained carrots and serve.

VARIATION: Add 1 teaspoon toasted SESAME SEEDS.

NUTRITIONAL INFORMATION:			
PER SERVE		PLAIN	SESAME SEEDS
FAT	TOTAL	1.3g	1.9g
	SATURATED	0.2g	0.3g
FIBRE		3.3g	3.4g
PROTEIN		0.8g	1.0g
CARBOHYDRATES		16.1g	16.1g
SODIUM		54mg	55mg
KILOJOULES		325 (cal 78)	350 (cal 83)

ALI'S FALAFELS

SERVES: 4

1 1/2 cups dried chickpeas

1/2 cup onion chopped

1/4 bunch fresh parsley

1 teaspoon crushed garlic (in jar)

1/2 teaspoon dried cumin

1 teaspoon salt

1/2 teaspoon black pepper

2 teaspoons baking powder

cooking spray

In a large bowl cover chickpeas with water and leave to soak for 24 hours. Blend garlic, onion and parsley in food processor for one minute. Add drained chickpeas, cumin, salt and pepper and process until smooth. Add baking powder and blend for 15 seconds. Place into a bowl and refrigerate for 1/2 hour then roll into 12 patties (3 per person). In a non-stick frypan that has been coated with cooking spray fry patties for about 2 minutes each side or until browned.

> *Dietitians Tip*   *This is a great high fibre,*
> *low GI recipe. For salt conscious people,*
> *reduce the salt to 1/2 teaspoon or omit altogether.*

NUTRITIONAL INFORMATION:

PER SERVE		
FAT	TOTAL	3.7g
	SATURATED	0.5g
FIBRE		8.8g
PROTEIN		11.2g
CARBOHYDRATES		23.3g
SODIUM		419mg
KILOJOULES		722 (cal 173)

FRIED RICE

SERVES: 6 As a side dish

2 cups raw long grain rice

3/4 cup shallots sliced

1/3 cup peas

1/2 cup lean short cut bacon diced

50g cooked peeled prawns

1 whole egg

1 egg white

1/4 cup skim milk

3 tablespoons soy sauce

cooking spray

Cook rice as instructed on back of rice packet, rinse and drain well. Spread out on tray and leave to dry for at least 1 hour. In a small bowl beat egg and egg white with milk. Coat a non-stick frypan with cooking spray and cook bacon, remove and leave to one side. Re-spray frypan and cook egg mix, remove from pan. Re-spray frypan again and add cooked rice, shallots, peas, prawns, cooked bacon and egg mix, combine well. Add in soy sauce and stir through mixture. Cook 3-4 minutes, stirring frequently.

VARIATION: For diabetics use DOONGARA or BASMATI rice

> *Dietitians Tip*   *A great dish using low GI rice as*
> *suggested in variation. To reduce the salt try using salt*
> *reduced soy sauce.*

NUTRITIONAL INFORMATION:

PER SERVE		
FAT	TOTAL	1.9g
	SATURATED	0.6g
FIBRE		2.2g
PROTEIN		11.4g
CARBOHYDRATES		55.8g
SODIUM		855mg
KILOJOULES		1209 (cal 288)

STUFFED MUSHROOMS

SERVES: 6 As a side dish

18 medium size mushrooms
1 cup cooked rice
$^1/_2$ cup tomato finely diced
$^1/_2$ cup onion finely diced
$^1/_2$ cup celery finely diced
$^1/_2$ cup capsicum finely diced
$^1/_2$ teaspoon crushed garlic (in jar)
1 tablespoon BBQ sauce
1 teaspoon worcestershire sauce
1 tablespoon tomato sauce
2 tablespoons parmesan cheese
$^1/_2$ cup grated 25% reduced fat tasty cheese
$^1/_2$ teaspoon dried oregano
$^1/_2$ teaspoon vegetable stock powder
cooking spray

Preheat oven to 180ºC fan forced.

In a large mixing bowl combine all ingredients except mushrooms and grated tasty cheese. Remove stem of mushrooms and spoon filling into each cap. Place each mushroom on a flat baking tray coated with cooking spray. Sprinkle a little cheese over each mushroom, bake for 25 minutes.

VARIATIONS:
Add in $^1/_3$ cup of short cut BACON finely diced to mixture or replace mushrooms with 3 large ZUCCHINIS. Cut zucchinis in half and scoop out soft centre, put stuffing into zucchinis and sprinkle cheese over top. Bake 35 minutes.

NUTRITIONAL INFORMATION:				
PER SERVE:		M/ROOM	BACON	ZUCCHINI
FAT	TOTAL	3.5g	3.9g	3.5g
	SATURATED	2.0g	2.1g	2.0g
FIBRE		3.2g	3.2g	2.5g
PROTEIN		6.8g	9.6g	5.8g
CARBOHYDRATES		11.7g	11.7g	11.8g
SODIUM		266mg	378mg	261mg
KILOJOULES		462 (cal 110)	505 (cal 120)	427 (cal 102)

VEGETABLE HOT POT

SERVES: 4 Large or 8 as a side dish

1 x 420g can 4 bean mix (drained and washed)
1 x 420g can corn kernels (drained)
2 x 425g cans crushed tomatoes
1 small onion diced
1 cup carrots sliced
1 cup celery sliced
1 cup capsicum diced
1 teaspoon crushed garlic (in jar)
2 teaspoons beef stock powder
1 teaspoon dried coriander
1 teaspoon dried turmeric
1 teaspoon dried cumin
cooking spray

In a large saucepan coated with cooking spray sauté onions, carrots, celery, capsicum and garlic for 3 minutes. Add cumin, coriander, turmeric and stock powder and cook 1 more minute. Add in beans, corn and tomatoes bring to boil and then simmer 5 minutes.

Dietitions Tip Packed with low GI ingredients such as corn and beans, this dish is a winner for people with diabetes.

NUTRITIONAL INFORMATION:			
PER SERVE		LARGE	S/DISH
FAT	TOTAL	2.0g	1.0g
	SATURATED	0.3g	0.2g
FIBRE		11.5g	5.8g
PROTEIN		10.0g	5.0g
CARBOHYDRATES		34.7g	17.3g
SODIUM		1037mg	519mg
KILOJOULES		823 (cal 197)	412 (cal 98)

ASPARAGUS WITH LEMON SAUCE

SERVES: 6 As a side dish

2 bunches fresh asparagus

1 cup evaporated light milk

2 tablespoons lemon juice

1 tablespoon plain flour

1 tablespoon reduced fat margarine (Flora® light)

$^1/_2$ teaspoon vegetable stock powder

pinch of dried tarragon

Melt margarine in a medium size saucepan, add flour and mix together. Gradually add in milk (using a whisk to avoid lumps). Add lemon juice, stock powder and tarragon, leave to one side while preparing asparagus. Cut thick ends off the asparagus spears, place in microwave with a little water for about 4 minutes or cook until firm but tender, drain. Pour sauce over asparagus and serve.

Dietitions Tip
A great dish. Perfect to serve with chicken or fish.

NUTRITIONAL INFORMATION:

PER SERVE		
FAT	TOTAL	2.0g
	SATURATED	0.9g
FIBRE		0.7g
PROTEIN		4.9g
CARBOHYDRATES		7.1g
SODIUM		127mg
KILOJOULES		283 (cal 68)

POTATO SLICE

SERVES: 6 As a side dish

3 large (650g) peeled potatoes

1 small onion finely diced

1 cup skim milk

1 whole egg

1 egg white

$^1/_2$ teaspoon crushed garlic (in jar)

$^1/_2$ teaspoon salt

2 tablespoons chopped parsley

$^3/_4$ cup grated 25% reduced fat tasty cheese

1 tablespoon parmesan cheese

pepper to taste

Preheat oven to 200°C fan forced.

In a large mixing bowl beat egg, egg white and milk together. Grate potatoes in a food processor. Combine all ingredients together except a third of a cup of grated cheese. Pour mixture into a quiche or pie dish coated with cooking spray and level top, sprinkle remaining cheese over and bake for 35-40 minutes or until browned.

Dietitions Tip *A family favourite that is low in fat but high in taste. Well done Annette!*

NUTRITIONAL INFORMATION:

PER SERVE		
FAT	TOTAL	4.5g
	SATURATED	2.5g
FIBRE		2.0g
PROTEIN		10.8g
CARBOHYDRATES		17.2g
SODIUM		300mg
KILOJOULES		645 (cal 154)

SALMON BAKE

SERVES: 6

1 x 415g can pink salmon (drained & mashed)
2 cups cooked macaroni noodles
1/2 cup onion finely diced
3/4 cup grated 25% reduced fat tasty cheese
1/2 cup frozen corn kernels
1/2 cup red capsicum small dice
1 cup skim milk
2 egg whites
1 whole egg
3 tablespoons chopped parsley
1/2 teaspoon dried dill
1 tablespoon lemon juice
cooking spray

Preheat oven to 180°C fan forced. In a large mixing bowl beat milk, egg whites and egg together. Add all other ingredients except the macaroni and cheese, mix well. Fold in the cooked macaroni noodles and two thirds of the cheese, combine together. Pour mixture into a quiche or pie dish that has been coated with cooking spray. Sprinkle remaining cheese over top. Bake 45 minutes or until browned and set in middle. Serve hot or cold.

NUTRITIONAL INFORMATION:

PER SERVE			PER SERVE	
FAT	TOTAL	8.6g	CARBOHYDRATE	14.7g
	SATURATED	3.5g	SODIUM	546mg
FIBRE		1.4g	KILOJOULES	988 (cal 236)
PROTEIN		24.7g		

SALMON RISSOLES

SERVES: 6

1 x 415g can pink salmon (drained & mashed)
1/2 cup shallots sliced
500g potato (about 5 medium) diced
1 1/2 cups carrots sliced
1 egg white
1 teaspoon salt
2 tablespoons chopped parsley
1 tablespoon lemon juice
cooking spray

In a large microwave dish cook potato and carrots until soft. Mash together in a large mixing bowl, add mashed salmon, lemon juice, shallots, egg white, parsley, salt and a little pepper to taste, combine ingredients together well. Refrigerate for a few hours if possible as this makes the mixture firmer for cooking. When ready to cook shape into 12 rissoles. Coat a non-stick frypan with cooking spray and fry for about 5 minutes on each side or until golden brown.

NUTRITIONAL INFORMATION:

PER SERVE		
FAT	TOTAL	4.6g
	SATURATED	1.3g
FIBRE		2.5g
PROTEIN		18.1g
CARBOHYDRATES		13.0g
SODIUM		703mg
KILOJOULES		705 (cal 168)

PRAWN & CRAB MORNAY

SERVES: 4

400g peeled green prawns
1 x 170g can crab meat undrained
80g seafood extender
1 x 375ml can evaporated light milk
2 tablespoons brandy
2 teaspoons fresh chopped coriander
2 teaspoons lemongrass (in jar)
1/2 cup grated 25% reduced fat tasty cheese
3 tablespoons corn flour
cooking spray

In a non-stick saucepan coated with cooking spray sauté prawns and brandy for 2 minutes. Combine corn flour and milk together, add to pan stirring continuously until boiled. Add crabmeat, seafood extender, coriander, lemongrass and cheese. When cheese has melted through mixture and has boiled serve over rice.

NUTRITIONAL INFORMATION:

PER SERVE		
FAT	TOTAL	5.4g
	SATURATED	3.5g
FIBRE		0g
PROTEIN		38.8g
CARBOHYDRATES		16.0g
SODIUM		980mg
KILOJOULES		1221 (cal 291)

TAHITIAN ATLANTIC SALMON

SERVES: 4

4 x 150g Atlantic salmon fillets

1 x 375ml can evaporated light milk

$^1/_4$ cup shallots sliced

2 teaspoons creole seasoning (Masterfoods® in jar)

4 tablespoons lime juice

1 teaspoon imitation coconut essence

1$^1/_2$ tablespoons corn flour

$^1/_2$ teaspoon vegetable stock powder

$^1/_2$ teaspoon crushed ginger (in jar)

Sprinkle creole seasoning over fillets. In a non-stick frypan generously coated with cooking spray fry salmon for about 4 minutes each side. In a small saucepan add juice, shallots, stock powder and ginger. Combine milk with corn flour and essence, add to pan whisking to avoid lumps. Bring to boil and serve over salmon.

VARIATION:
Replace salmon with 4 x 150g FISH FILLETS of your choice

> *Dietitions Tip* This is a great dish as salmon is
> a good source of healthy omega 3 fats.

NUTRITIONAL INFORMATION:

PER SERVE		SALMON	FISH
FAT	TOTAL	6.8g	4.8g
	SATURATED	1.5g	3.2g
FIBRE		0.1g	0.1g
PROTEIN		38.0g	39.3g
CARBOHYDRATES		15.6g	15.6g
SODIUM		303mg	435 mg
KILOJOULES		1208 (cal 287)	1161 (cal 277)

SEAFOOD CHOWDER

SERVES: 6

300g boneless fish fillets cut into pieces

100g peeled green prawns

1 x 170g can crab meat undrained

50g seafood extender

1 x 375ml can evaporated light milk

2 cups skim milk

2 cups water

$^1/_2$ cup white wine

1 tablespoon fish sauce

$^1/_2$ cup shallots chopped

1 teaspoon crushed garlic (in jar)

2 tablespoons chopped parsley

6 tablespoons corn flour

salt and pepper to taste

In a large boiler place water, wine, garlic and fish sauce. Bring to boil, add fish and cook 2 minutes. Add shallots, prawns, seafood extender, crabmeat and parsley. Simmer 5 minutes. In a cup combine $^1/_2$ cup of the skim milk with corn flour until blended, leave to one side. In another saucepan place remaining 1$^1/_2$ cups of skim milk and whole can of evaporated milk to pan. Once boiled add to boiler (I have done it this way as the milk will scorch if you boil it with the seafood), now add in remaining milk/corn flour mix to pot and bring to boil. Remove quickly so as not to let the bottom of the pan scorch. Salt and pepper to taste.

NUTRITIONAL INFORMATION:

PER SERVE		
FAT	TOTAL	2.8g
	SATURATED	1.7g
FIBRE		0.1g
PROTEIN		26.6g
CARBOHYDRATES		21.5g
SODIUM		706mg
KILOJOULES		975 (cal 233)

CHILLI PRAWNS

SERVES: 4

500g peeled green prawns

$^1/_2$ cup sweet chilli sauce

1 cup evaporated light milk

$^1/_2$ cup shallots or onion sliced

1 teaspoon crushed garlic (in jar)

1 teaspoon crushed ginger (in jar)

2 teaspoons fish sauce

2 teaspoons soy sauce

2 tablespoons corn flour

cooking spray

In a non-stick saucepan coated with cooking spray sauté ginger, garlic and prawns for 2 minutes. Toss in shallots and cook 30 seconds. Add fish, soy and chilli sauces to pan. Mix corn flour with milk, pour into pan and bring to boil stirring continuously. Serve with rice or pasta.

VARIATIONS:
Replace prawns with either 500g skinless CHICKEN BREAST strips
or 500g lean BEEF strips.

> **Dietitions Tip** *Everyone will love this delicious recipe. Serve this with Basmati or Doongara rice.*

NUTRITIONAL INFORMATION:

PER SERVE		PRAWN	CHICKEN	BEEF
FAT	TOTAL	2.6g	4.8g	6.5g
	SATURATED	1.3g	1.9g	3.2g
FIBRE		1.7g	1.7g	1.7g
PROTEIN		31.6g	34.2g	33.0g
CARBOHYDRATES		18.3g	18.3g	18.3g
SODIUM		1201mg	832mg	836mg
KILOJOULES		950 (cal 227)	1072 (cal 256)	1113 (cal 266)

FISH WITH PARSLEY & ONION SAUCE

SERVES: 4

4 x 125g boneless fish fillets

2 cups skim milk

$^1/_3$ cup finely chopped parsley

$^1/_2$ cup onion finely diced

2 tablespoons reduced fat margarine (Flora® light)

2 tablespoons plain flour

1 teaspoon chicken stock powder

salt and pepper to taste

In a medium size saucepan melt margarine and sauté onion for 1 minute. Add flour and cook 30 seconds. Slowly add in milk using a whisk to avoid lumps. Add stock powder, parsley, salt and pepper. In a large non-stick frypan generously coated with cooking spray cook fish pieces. Pour sauce over fish and serve.

VARIATIONS:
Replace fish with 750g raw lean CORNED SILVERSIDE, once cooked allow 125g per serve
or 500g raw TRIPE cut into strips.

> **Dietitions Tip** *This quick and easy recipe makes it easy to include 2-3 fish meals per week.*

NUTRITIONAL INFORMATION:

PER SERVE		FISH	CORN/SIL	TRIPE
FAT	TOTAL	6.5g	8.5g	6.7g
	SATURATED	2.3g	3.1g	2.0g
FIBRE		0.6g	0.6g	0.6g
PROTEIN		31.7g	36.1g	22.2g
CARBOHYDRATES		11.5g	11.5g	11.5g
SODIUM		430mg	3395mg	445mg
KILOJOULES		1006 (cal 240)	1114 (cal 266)	813 (cal 192)

Chicken

CHICKEN LAKSA

SERVES: 4

400g skinless chicken breast diced

1/2 cup carrot cut into thin strips

1/2 cup capsicum cut into thin strips

I cup bean sprouts

1/2 cup shallots sliced

I tablespoon fresh chopped coriander

1/2 teaspoon crushed garlic (in jar)

I teaspoon crushed ginger (in jar)

I teaspoon lemongrass (in jar)

3 teaspoons massaman curry paste

I teaspoon turmeric

I teaspoon imitation coconut essence

I x 375ml can evaporated light milk

500 ml carton chicken stock liquid
(ready made)

I tablespoon corn flour

1 1/2 cups singapore noodles

cooking spray

In a large non-stick frypan or wok coated with cooking spray sauté chicken, garlic and ginger together for 4 minutes. Toss in carrots and capsicum and cook another 2 minutes. Place all other ingredients except milk and corn flour into pan and mix together well. Combine cornflour with milk and add to dish. Simmer 5 minutes then serve.

VARIATIONS: *Replace chicken with 400g lean BEEF strips or 400g raw PEELED PRAWNS or 300g diced TOFU.*

Dietitions Tip *Noodles have a low GI, making this dish ideal for people with diabetes.*

NUTRITIONAL INFORMATION:

PER SERVE		CHICKEN	BEEF	PRAWN	TOFU
FAT	TOTAL	5.0g	6.5g	3.4g	7.3g
	SATURATED	2.2g	3.1g	1.7g	1.5g
FIBRE		1.7g	1.7g	1.7g	1.7g
PROTEIN		35.3g	34.3g	33.2g	20.2g
CARBOHYDRATES		27.2g	27.3g	27.3g	30.2g
SODIUM		828mg	831mg	1123mg	778mg
KILOJOULES		1252 (cal 299)	1285 (cal 307)	1154 (cal 275)	1049 (cal 251)

CHICKEN BURGER

SERVES: 6

500g very lean chicken mince

I egg white

1/2 teaspoon crushed garlic (in jar)

1/2 cup onion or shallots finely diced

1/2 cup breadcrumbs (packet)

1/2 teaspoon dried basil

2 tablespoons sweet chilli sauce

cooking spray

In a large mixing bowl combine all the ingredients and mix really well. Shape into 6 patties and place into a non-stick frypan coated with cooking spray. Cook 3 minutes each side or until cooked.

Serve in a bun with salad or with vegies, mash and gravy.

TIP: To know if chicken mince is lean, look for the least amount of white pieces in the mince. If the mince has a lot of these white pieces it means it has skin in it as well, which makes the mince very high in fat.

NUTRITIONAL INFORMATION

PER SERVE		BURGER ONLY	BURGER + BUN
FAT	TOTAL	2.5g	4.8g
	SATURATED	0.6g	1.2g
FIBRE		0.9g	3.7g
PROTEIN		21.0g	29.7g
CARBOHYDRATES		8.2g	51.7g
SODIUM		213mg	843mg
KILOJOULES		588 (cal 140)	1560 (cal 372)

Dietitions Tip *A family favourite, serve on multigrain rolls with lots of salad for a complete meal.*

CHICKEN IN PLUM SAUCE

SERVES: 4

600g skinless chicken breast
1 small onion thinly sliced
1 teaspoon crushed garlic (in jar)
$^1/_2$ cup capsicum thinly sliced
$^1/_2$ cup celery thinly sliced
$^1/_2$ cup carrot thinly sliced
$^1/_2$ cup snow peas cut in half
$^1/_3$ cup spicy plum sauce (in jar)
1 teaspoon chicken stock powder
1 tablespoon soy sauce
1 tablespoon corn flour
$^1/_2$ cup water
cooking spray

Cut vegetables as described above. Dice chicken and sauté with garlic in a wok or frypan coated with cooking spray. When nearly cooked add all vegetables and cook for 3-4 minutes or until vegetables are cooked to your liking. Place stock powder, soy sauce and plum sauce into pan, blend corn flour with water and add stirring continuously, bring to boil then reduce to a simmer for 2 minutes. Serve with rice, pasta or noodles.

VARIATIONS:

Replace chicken with 600g NEW FASHIONED PORK cut into strips or diced.

NUTRITIONAL INFORMATION:		
PER SERVE	CHICKEN	PORK
FAT TOTAL	4.0g	2.0g
SATURATED	1.0g	0.6g
FIBRE	1.7g	1.7g
PROTEIN	35.6g	38.2g
CARBOHYDRATES	17.2g	17.2g
SODIUM	1069mg	1064mg
KILOJOULES	1036 (cal 247)	1011 (cal 241)

HAWAIIAN CHICKEN

SERVES: 4

500g skinless chicken breast
$^1/_2$ cup short cut bacon diced
1 cup capsicum sliced
1 cup onion sliced
$^1/_2$ cup fresh tomatoes chopped
1 tablespoon tomato paste
$^3/_4$ cup canned pineapple pieces (in natural juice)
1$^1/_2$ cups pineapple juice (no sugar added)
2 teaspoons chicken stock powder
1 teaspoon crushed garlic (in jar)
$^1/_4$ teaspoon imitation coconut essence
$^3/_4$ cup evaporated light milk
3 tablespoons corn flour
cooking spray

Dice chicken. Prepare vegetables as described. In a non-stick frypan coated with cooking spray brown bacon, remove and leave to one side. Re-spray frypan and sauté chicken and garlic for 3 minutes. Add onion and capsicum and cook 1 minute. Add tomato, drained pineapple pieces (cut pieces in half), pineapple juice, tomato paste and chicken stock powder, combine well, bring to boil and simmer 5 minutes or until vegetables are cooked to your liking, add bacon. Combine corn flour, coconut essence and milk, add to mixture, bring to boil and serve.

VARIATIONS:
Replace chicken with 500g lean BEEF in strips,
or 400g TOFU diced.

NUTRITIONAL INFORMATION:

PER SERVE		CHICKEN	BEEF	TOFU
TOTAL	FAT	4.7g	6.5g	7.9g
	SATURATED	1.8g	3.1g	1.1g
FIBRE		1.7g	1.7g	1.7g
PROTEIN		36.8g	35.5g	18.5g
CARBOHYDRATES		31.5g	32.5g	36.5g
SODIUM		791mg	794mg	728mg
KILOJOULES		1341 (cal 321)	1382 (cal 330)	1110 (cal 265)

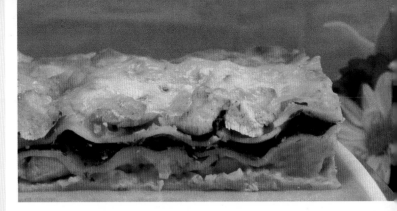

CHICKEN & SPINACH LASAGNE

SERVES: 6

600g skinless chicken breast diced
1 cup onion diced
1 teaspoon crushed garlic (in jar)
1 pkt (45g) chicken soup mix
2 cups skim milk
1 tablespoon reduced fat margarine (Flora® light)
2 tablespoons plain flour
1/4 teaspoon dried tarragon
1 x 250g pkt frozen spinach
250g tub low fat cottage cheese
1/2 cup grated 25% reduced fat tasty cheese
9 lasagne sheets
cooking spray

Preheat oven to 180°C fan forced.

Defrost spinach, then squeeze water out of spinach and place in a bowl. In a food processor blend cottage cheese until smooth, add this to the spinach and fold together, leave to one side. In a non-stick frypan coated with cooking spray sauté chicken, onion and garlic until nearly cooked. In a separate saucepan melt margarine, add in flour and combine. Slowly add milk using a whisk to avoid lumps, add dry soup mix into milk mixture with tarragon. When boiled pour over chicken and mix together. Coat a lasagne dish (about 15cm x 28cm) with cooking spray then place 3 lasagne sheets on bottom of dish, spoon half the chicken mixture over lasagne then top with 3 more lasagne sheets. Spread spinach mixture on top of sheets, then top with the remaining lasagne sheets. Spoon remaining chicken over top, sprinkle cheese over and cover with foil (give the foil a coating of cooking spray so cheese doesn't stick too much). Bake for 40 minutes then remove foil and cook a further 10-15 minutes to brown top.

Dietitions Tip *Pasta is a great low GI food that makes this dish a winner for people with diabetes.*

NUTRITIONAL INFORMATION:

PER SERVE		
FAT	TOTAL	8.9g
	SATURATED	2.5g
FIBRE		3.4g
PROTEIN		42.4g
CARBOHYDRATES		36.0g
SODIUM		691mg
KILOJOULES		1669 (cal 399)

HONEY SOY CHICKEN

SERVES: 6

600g skinless chicken breast

2 cups zucchini sliced

1 1/2 cups carrots sliced

1 1/2 cups fresh beans sliced

1 cup shallots sliced

1 teaspoon crushed garlic (in jar)

1 teaspoon crushed ginger (in jar)

1 tablespoon honey

3 tablespoons sweet soy sauce

1 tablespoon soy sauce

2 teaspoons chicken stock powder

1 tablespoon corn flour

1 1/2 cups water

cooking spray

Cut chicken into strips. Prepare vegetables as described above. In a large frypan or wok (which has a lid) coated with cooking spray sauté chicken, garlic and ginger together for 4 minutes. Toss in beans, zucchini and carrots and cook with lid on for a further 4 minutes or until vegetables are cooked to your liking stirring occasionally. Add shallots, soy sauces, honey and chicken stock. Mix cornflour with water and add to pot, bring to boil.

VARIATIONS:
Replace chicken with 600g lean BEEF strips
or 600g BUTTERFLY PORK STEAKS cut into strips
or 600g lean LEG LAMB STEAKS cut into strips or 400g TOFU diced.

Dietitions Tip To reduce the salt in this dish, try using salt reduced soy sauce.

NUTRITIONAL INFORMATION:

PER SERVE		CHICKEN	BEEF	PORK	LAMB	TOFU
FAT	TOTAL	2.7g	4.1g	1.4g	2.6g	4.4g
	SATURATED	0.7g	1.7g	0.4g	1.1g	0.1g
FIBRE		2.4g	2.4g	2.4g	2.4g	2.4g
PROTEIN		24.7g	23.7g	26.5g	24.9g	8.8g
CARBOHYDRATES		12.2g	12.2g	12.2g	12.2g	14.9g
SODIUM		1065mg	1068mg	1062mg	1074mg	1014mg
KILOJOULES		734 (cal 173)	757 (cal 181)	707 (cal 169)	724 (cal 173)	491 (cal 117)

CREOLE CHICKEN

SERVES: 6

600g skinless chicken breast

1 cup celery sliced

1 cup yellow squash quartered

1 cup carrot diced

1 cup capsicum diced

1 cup onion diced

1 x 425g can crushed tomatoes

1 x 810g can whole peeled tomatoes

2 tablespoons tomato paste

1/2 cup white wine

2 teaspoons chicken stock powder

1 teaspoon crushed garlic (in jar)

2 teaspoons paprika

1 teaspoon dried cumin

1/2 teaspoon dried thyme

2 teaspoons curry powder

1 teaspoon imitation coconut essence

3/4 cup evaporated light milk

1 tablespoon corn flour

cooking spray

Dice chicken. Prepare vegetables as described above. In a large saucepan that has been coated with cooking spray sauté chicken and garlic together for 3 minutes. Add paprika, cumin, thyme, curry powder and stock powder to pan and cook 1 minute. Add vegetables and wine, toss through mix. Add both cans of tomatoes and tomato paste, bring to boil and simmer 5 minutes or until vegetables are cooked to your liking. Combine corn flour, coconut essence and milk together, add to mixture, bring to boil and serve.

VARIATIONS:
Replace chicken with 600g lean BEEF cut in strips or 600g lean LAMB LEG STEAKS cut into strips or 400g TOFU diced.

NUTRITIONAL INFORMATION:

PER SERVE		CHICKEN	BEEF	LAMB	TOFU
FAT	TOTAL	3.8g	5.3g	3.8g	5.6
	SATURATED	1.2g	2.2g	1.6g	0.6
FIBRE		5.1g	5.1g	5.1g	5.1
PROTEIN		29.0g	28.0g	29.1g	13.9
CARBOHYDRATES		16.9g	16.9g	16.9g	19.6
SODIUM		586mg	589mg	595mg	535m
KILOJOULES		974 (cal 232)	1008 (cal 241)	975 (cal 233)	742 (cal 177

MEXICANA CHICKEN

SERVES: 6

500g skinless chicken breast diced

1 cup onion sliced

1 cup capsicum sliced

1 x 415g can diced tomatoes

1 x 450g can refried beans

1 teaspoon crushed garlic (in jar)

2 teaspoons dried cumin

2 teaspoons paprika

2 teaspoons dried oregano

1/4 teaspoon chilli powder (or to taste)

2 teaspoons chicken stock powder

cooking spray

TO MAKE TORTILLA BASKETS AS IN PICTURE:
Coat an ovenproof dessert bowl with cooking spray, press a large tortilla into bowl, coat with cooking spray and bake in oven 180°C for about 10 minutes. Leave to cool in bowl.

VARIATIONS:
Replace chicken with lean BEEF strips,
or to make VEGETARIAN replace chicken with 2 cans drained and washed KIDNEY BEANS and replace chicken stock powder with VEGETABLE STOCK POWDER.

In a large saucepan coated with cooking spray sauté chicken and garlic for 4 minutes, add onion and capsicum and cook 2 minutes. Add cumin, paprika, oregano, chilli powder and stock powder, cook 1 minute. Add tomatoes and refried beans, combine well. When boiled simmer for 1 minute then serve.

NUTRITIONAL INFORMATION:				
PER SERVE		CHICKEN	BEEF	VEGETARIAN
FAT	TOTAL	2.9g	4.0g	1.5g
	SATURATED	0.6g	1.4g	0.2g
FIBRE		5.2g	5.2g	11.4g
PROTEIN		24.1g	23.3g	11.5g
CARBOHYDRATES		16.2g	16.2g	28.6g
SODIUM		752mg	754mg	1007mg
KILOJOULES		770 (cal 184)	797 (cal 190)	717 (cal 171)

BEEF TORTILLA STACK

SERVES: 8

750g lean beef mince

5 tortilla sheets

$^1/_2$ cup grated 25% reduced fat tasty cheese

1 cup onion finely diced

1 teaspoon crushed garlic (in jar)

$^1/_2$ cup corn kernels

1 cup small capsicum diced

1 x 425g can crushed tomatoes

3 tablespoons tomato paste

1$^1/_2$ cups water

1 teaspoon beef stock powder

1 x 35g pkt taco seasoning (Old El Paso®)

cooking spray

Preheat oven to 180°C fan forced.

In a large saucepan coated with cooking spray sauté mince. When cooked drain and place in a bowl, leave to one side. Add all the remaining ingredients to saucepan except the tortilla sheets and cheese. Bring mixture to boil, simmer 10 minutes. Remove 1 cup of the tomato sauce and leave to one side (this will go on the top). Add the mince to remaining sauce and bring to boil. Coat a quiche or pie plate (23cm) with cooking spray and lay 1 tortilla sheet on base and spread 1$^1/_2$ cups of mince sauce over sheet, repeat this 3 times. Top with last tortilla sheet and cover with reserved tomato sauce, sprinkle cheese over top. Bake for 30 minutes or until cheese has browned.

VARIATIONS:
Replace lean beef mince with 750g lean CHICKEN MINCE, or for a VEGETARIAN version replace mince with 1 x 450g can REFRIED BEANS and 1 x 425g can KIDNEY BEANS drained and washed. Combine both beans with tomato sauce mix and layer as you would the mince sauce.

Dietitians Tip   A tasty mexican feast minus the fat!

NUTRITIONAL INFORMATION:

PER SERVE		BEEF	CHICKEN	VEGETARIAN
FAT	TOTAL	7.6g	6.3g	4.6g
	SATURATED	3.5g	2.6g	2.0g
FIBRE		3.3g	3.3g	8.0g
PROTEIN		28.5g	29.5g	12.9g
CARBOHYDRATES		23.9g	23.9g	36.4g
SODIUM		1008mg	1005mg	1311mg
KILOJOULES		1173 (cal 280)	1142 (cal 273)	1002 (cal 239)

SPICY APRICOT LAMB CASSEROLE

SERVES: 4

500g lean lamb leg steak

$^1/_2$ cup dried apricots

2$^1/_2$ cups apricot nectar

2 teaspoons beef stock powder

1 cup onion diced

1 cup carrot sliced

1 cup celery sliced

1 x 300ml jar medium salsa (Masterfoods®)

1 teaspoon curry powder

1 cup water

$^1/_4$ cup plain flour

Preheat oven to 180°C fan forced.

Dice lamb. Prepare vegetables and cut dried apricots in half. Coat lamb in flour and place in a non-stick frypan that has been generously coated with cooking spray, toss meat in pan until browned on the outside (this will seal in the juices.) In a large casserole dish (that has a lid) place all ingredients, stirring together until combined. Place lid on casserole dish and cook in oven for 1$^1/_2$ hours or until vegetables are cooked to your liking.

VARIATIONS:
Replace lamb with 500g diced skinless CHICKEN BREAST or with 500g lean BEEF diced.

NUTRITIONAL INFORMATION:

PER SERVE		LAMB	CHICKEN	BEEF
FAT	TOTAL	5.1g	5.3g	7.0g
	SATURATED	1.6g	1.1g	3.8g
FIBRE		3.8g	3.8g	3.8g
PROTEIN		32.9g	32.6g	31.4g
CARBOHYDRATES		45.5g	45.5g	45.5g
SODIUM		972mg	961mg	965mg
KILOJOULES		1482 (cal 354)	1482 (cal 354)	1524 (cal 364)

MONGOLIAN LAMB

SERVES: 4

600g lean lamb leg steak
1 cup onion sliced
1 cup capsicum sliced
1 cup water
1 teaspoon crushed ginger (in jar)
1 teaspoon crushed garlic (in jar)
1 tablespoon hoi sin sauce
2 tablespoons soy sauce
1 tablespoon oyster sauce
2 teaspoons sesame seeds
1 teaspoon beef stock powder
1 teaspoon sugar
2 tablespoons corn flour
cooking spray

Cut lamb into strips. In a non-stick frypan or wok coated with cooking spray sauté lamb, ginger and garlic until meat is nearly cooked. Add onion and capsicum and cook a further 2 minutes. Combine cornflour with water and add to pan with all other remaining ingredients. Bring to boil then serve with rice or noodles.

VARIATIONS:
Replace lamb with 600g lean BEEF strips
or skinless CHICKEN BREAST cut into strips

> *Dietitions Tip* This dish is a bit high in salt so look for salt reduced Asian sauces. People with diabetes enjoy in moderation.

NUTRITIONAL INFORMATION:

PER SERVE		LAMB	BEEF	CHICKEN
FAT	TOTAL	4.5g	6.8g	4.7g
	SATURATED	1.7g	2.6g	1.1g
FIBRE		1.5g	1.5g	1.5g
PROTEIN		36.9g	35.1g	36.2g
CARBOHYDRATES		8.5g	8.5g	8.5g
SODIUM		1323mg	1314mg	1309mg
KILOJOULES		986 (cal 235)	1035 (cal 246)	986 (cal 234)

VEAL WITH CREAMY MUSHROOM SAUCE

SERVES: 4

4 x 150g lean veal steaks
500g mushrooms (quartered)
2 sachets Lite Mushroom & Chive Cup-A-Soup®
1/2 cup shallots sliced
2 tablespoons chopped parsley
2 tablespoons brandy
1 x 375ml can evaporated light milk
1 teaspoon crushed garlic (in jar)
1 tablespoon corn flour
cooking spray

In a non-stick saucepan that has been coated with cooking spray sauté mushrooms, brandy and garlic together for 2 minutes. Combine corn flour and soup mix with milk and add to saucepan with parsley and shallots. Bring to boil and simmer until mushrooms are cooked to your liking. Leave to one side. In a non-stick frypan coated with cooking spray, fry steaks until cooked to your liking. Pour sauce over veal and serve.

VARIATIONS:
Replace veal with 600g lean BEEF STEAKS
or 600g skinless CHICKEN BREASTS
or 400g TOFU cut into large slices

> *Dietitions Tip* A creamy mushroom sauce without all the fat! Serve this delicious recipe with pasta or rice.

NUTRITIONAL INFORMATION:

PER SERVE		VEAL	BEEF	CHICKEN	TOFU
FAT	TOTAL	5.0g	8.4g	6.3g	8.8g
	SATURATED	2.1g	3.9g	2.4g	1.5g
FIBRE		4.2g	4.2g	4.2g	4.2g
PROTEIN		46.4g	45.4g	46.8g	22.9g
CARBOHYDRATES		15.8g	15.8g	15.8g	19.8g
SODIUM		637mg	588mg	583mg	507mg
KILOJOULES		1373 (cal 328)	1472 (cal 352)	1423 (cal 340)	1074 (cal 256)

SWEET & SPICY LAMB

SERVES: 6

600g lean lamb leg steak
1 cup diced apple peeled
$\frac{1}{2}$ cup sultanas
$\frac{1}{2}$ cup almond slivers
1 cup onion sliced
1 teaspoon crushed ginger (in jar)
1 teaspoon crushed garlic (in jar)
1 x 375ml can evaporated light milk
$\frac{1}{2}$ teaspoon imitation coconut essence
1 teaspoon dried cardamon
1 teaspoon dried cumin
1 teaspoon dried coriander
1 teaspoon dried turmeric
2 teaspoons beef stock powder
1 tablespoon tomato paste
1 tablespoon corn flour
cooking spray

Cut lamb into strips. Toast almonds on a sheet of foil placed under the griller until browned, leave to one side. In a non-stick frypan or wok that has been coated with cooking spray sauté lamb, ginger and garlic until meat is nearly cooked. Add onion, apple and sultanas and cook 2 minutes more. Put cardamon, cumin, coriander, turmeric, stock powder and tomato paste into pan. Mix corn flour into milk with essence, add to frypan, stirring continuously until boiled. Sprinkle almonds over top and serve with rice, couscous or potato.

VARIATIONS: Replace lamb with 600g lean BEEF strips or 600g skinless CHICKEN BREAST cut into strips or 400g TOFU diced or reduce fat count per person by 2.3g by OMITTING ALMONDS

NUTRITIONAL INFORMATION:

PER SERVE		LAMB	CHICKEN	BEEF	TOFU
FAT	TOTAL	5.0g	5.1g	6.5g	6.8g
	SATURATED	1.2g	0.8g	1.8g	1.8g
FIBRE		1.8g	1.8g	1.8g	1.8g
PROTEIN		24.8g	24.6g	23.6g	8.7g
CARBOHYDRATES		18.0g	18.0g	18.0g	20.6g
SODIUM1		396mg	387mg	390mg	336mg
KILOJOULES		892 (cal 213)	892 (cal 213)	925 (cal 221)	660 (cal 157)

PORCUPINE CASSEROLE

SERVES: 4

MEAT BALLS
600g lean beef mince
$\frac{1}{3}$ cup raw long grain rice
1 teaspoon beef stock powder
1 egg white

SAUCE
1 x 420g can tomato soup
1 x 425g can crushed tomatoes
$\frac{1}{2}$ cup onion finely diced
1 cup water
2 teaspoons beef stock powder
1 teaspoon dried oregano
1 teaspoon crushed garlic (in jar)

Preheat oven to 190°C fan forced.

In a large casserole dish (that has a lid) combine all ingredients listed to make the sauce. Pour into casserole dish and leave to one side. In a medium size mixing bowl combine all ingredients listed to make meat balls. Using your hands mix together well. Shape into 12 round meat balls, add to casserole dish and bake for 1 hour.

VARIATIONS:
Replace lean beef mince with either 600g lean CHICKEN MINCE
or 600g lean PORK MINCE

Dietitions Tip   A hearty meal for the whole family. To reduce the salt in this dish look for no added salt tomatoes.

NUTRITIONAL INFORMATION:

PER SERVE		BEEF	CHICKEN	PORK
FAT	TOTAL	6.6g	4.5g	3.4g
	SATURATED	2.6g	1.1g	0.9g
FIBRE		4.1g	4.1g	4.1g
PROTEIN		37.0g	38.5g	38.5g
CARBOHYDRATES		29.7g	29.7g	29.7g
SODIUM		1531mg	1526mg	1542mg
KILOJOULES		1369 (cal 326)	1319 (cal 315)	1280 (cal 305)

SATAY PORK

SERVES: 6

6 x 100g new fashioned butterfly pork steaks

12 bamboo skewers

SAUCE

$^1/_4$ cup crunchy peanut butter

$^1/_3$ cup onion finely diced

1 teaspoon crushed garlic

1 tablespoon soy sauce

1 teaspoon dried coriander

$^1/_2$ teaspoon dried cumin

$^1/_2$ teaspoon dried turmeric

$^1/_4$ teaspoon chilli powder (optional)

$^3/_4$ cup evaporated light milk

$^1/_2$ teaspoon coconut essence

SAUCE: Coat a small non-stick saucepan with cooking spray, sauté garlic and onion for 2 minutes. Add all other ingredients combining together well, bring to boil, leave to one side.

Cut each pork slice into two long strips. Weave each strip onto a bamboo skewer and grill until cooked. Pour sauce over each stick.

VARIATIONS:
Replace pork with either 600g of skinless CHICKEN BREAST or 600g lean BEEF, or 600g lean LAMB LEG STEAKS, or 600g GREEN PRAWNS, or 400g TOFU large cubes

Dietitions Tip A satay sauce that is low in fat but high in taste. Well done Annette!

NUTRITIONAL INFORMATION:

PER SERVE		PORK	CHICKEN	BEEF	LAMB	PRAWN	TOFU
FAT	TOTAL	5.8g	7.1g	8.5g	7.0g	5.4g	8.8g
	SATURATED	1.5g	1.8g	2.8g	2.2g	1.3g	1.2g
FIBRE		1.1g	1.1g	1.1g	1.1g	1.1g	2.1g
PROTEIN		29.7g	27.9g	26.9g	28.1g	25.8g	12.0g
CARBOHYDRATES		5.5g	5.5g	5.5g	5.5g	5.5g	8.1g
SODIUM		318mg	321mg	324mg	330mg	616mg	270mg
KILOJOULES		810 (cal 193)	827 (cal 198)	860 (cal 205)	827 (cal 198)	729 (cal 174)	595 (cal 142)

BEEF IN BLACK BEAN

SERVES: 4

450g lean beef strips

1 bunch fresh asparagus

1/2 cup red capsicum diced

1/2 cup green capsicum diced

1 cup celery sliced

1 cup onion sliced

3 tablespoons black bean sauce (bottled)

1 teaspoon crushed garlic (in jar)

2 teaspoons beef stock powder

1 teaspoon sugar

2 teaspoons corn flour

1 cup water

Trim about 5 cms from thick end of asparagus spears then cut spears 3-4 cm in size, leave to one side. In a non-stick frypan or wok coated with cooking spray sauté garlic and beef strips until cooked. Remove from pan. Re-spray pan and cook capsicum, celery, onion and asparagus, toss together for 1 minute. Place lid on pan and cook for 3 minutes, stirring occasionally. Add cooked beef to vegetables, add stock powder, sugar and black bean sauce, toss ingredients together. Blend cornflour with water and add to frypan, stirring through. When boiled serve over rice or noodles.

VARIATIONS:
Replace beef with 450g skinless CHICKEN BREAST cut into strips or 450g NEW FASHIONED PORK STEAKS cut into strips or 450g lean LAMB LEG STEAKS cut into strips

Dietitions Tip A great tasting dish, serve with a low GI rice like Doongara or noodles to make it a meal everyone will enjoy.

NUTRITIONAL INFORMATION:				
PER SERVE		BEEF	CHICKEN	PORK	LAMB
FAT	TOTAL	5.9g	4.3g	2.9g	4.2g
	SATURATED	2.4g	1.3g	1.0g	1.7g
FIBRE		2.3g	2.3g	2.3g	2.3g
PROTEIN		28.0g	29.1g	31.1g	29.3g
CARBOHYDRATES		7.9g	7.9g	7.9g	7.9g
SODIUM		654mg	651mg	648mg	661mg
KILOJOULES		823 (cal 196)	786 (cal 187)	767 (cal 183)	786 (cal 187)

POTATO MEAT PIE

SERVES: 6

PASTRY
³/4 cup plain flour

¹/4 cup self raising flour

1 egg white

2 tablespoons reduced fat margarine (Flora® light)

2 tablespoons skim milk

extra flour to roll pastry

MEAT FILLING
500g lean beef mince

³/4 cup onion finely diced

2 tablespoons tomato sauce

2 tablespoons BBQ sauce

1 tablespoon oyster sauce

1 teaspoon worcestershire sauce

2 teaspoons beef stock powder

6 tablespoons light Gravox® powder

1 ¹/2 cups water

pepper to taste

POTATO TOP
5 cups potatoes (about 750g) peeled and diced

¹/3 cup grated 25% reduced fat tasty cheese

¹/4 cup skim milk

1 teaspoon reduced fat margarine (Flora® light)

¹/4 teaspoon salt

Preheat oven to 190° C fan forced.

PASTRY: Place flour into a medium size mixing bowl. Melt margarine and add milk. Using a fork beat egg white into milk until combined, pour into flour and fold together. Place pastry on a well floured surface and roll out to fit shape of round pie dish (23cm) coated with cooking spray. Using a rolling pin, roll up pastry, lift onto pie plate. Trim around edges and bake 10-15 minutes or until lightly browned. Leave to one side.

MEAT FILLING: In a non-stick frypan cook mince, drain off any liquid, add onion. Cook together for 2 minutes, add all other ingredients listed for the meat filling. Bring to boil stirring constantly. Leave on lowest heat until pastry and potato are ready.

POTATO TOP: Microwave diced potato in a little water until cooked (about 12-15 minutes). When cooked drain, mash with milk, margarine and salt.

ASSEMBLING PIE: Spoon meat filling over pastry in pie dish then top with mashed potato. Sprinkle grated cheese over top and bake for 30 minutes or until top has browned.

Dietitions Tip For people with diabetes, this is a little high in salt so enjoy in moderation.

NUTRITIONAL INFORMATION:

PER SERVE		
FAT	TOTAL	7.6g
	SATURATED	2.7g
FIBRE		3.4g
PROTEIN		27.5g
CARBOHYDRATES		46.8g
SODIUM		1605mg
KILOJOULES		1544 (cal 368)

BEEF STEW WITH PARSLEY DUMPLINGS

SERVES: 6

STEW
600g lean beef diced
4 cups water
1½ cups choko diced
1 cup celery sliced
2 cups carrots sliced
1 cup onion diced
1 teaspoon crushed garlic (in jar)
2 teaspoons beef stock powder
1 teaspoon worcestershire sauce
3 bay leaves
1 x 40g pkt French onion soup
1 tablespoon corn flour
¼ cup water
cooking spray

DUMPLINGS
1¾ cups self raising flour
2 tablespoons chopped parsley
1 teaspoon beef stock powder
⅔ cup skim milk
1 egg white
extra flour for shaping dumplings

DUMPLINGS: In a medium size mixing bowl mix together all the dumpling ingredients. Using a little extra flour for shaping, roll dough in hands to shape into 12 dumplings (round balls), leave to one side.

STEW: In a large boiler (that has a lid) coated with cooking spray, brown meat, onion, garlic, choko, celery and carrots tossing frequently for 5 minutes. Add stock powder, water, worcestershire sauce, bay leaves and soup mix, combine well. Bring to boil then gently put dumplings on top of stew mix, put lid on and simmer for about 40 minutes. Combine cornflour and water. When cooked gently remove dumplings and thicken stew with corn flour mix, bring to boil. When serving place 2 dumplings on top of each serve.

VARIATIONS:
Replace beef with 600g skinless CHICKEN BREAST diced or 600g lean LEG LAMB STEAKS diced.

Dietitions Tip   A hearty and healthy stew the whole family will love.

NUTRITIONAL INFORMATION:

PER SERVE		BEEF	CHICKEN	LAMB
FAT	TOTAL	4.7g	3.3g	3.2g
	SATURATED	1.8g	0.8g	1.2g
FIBRE		3.6g	3.6g	3.6g
PROTEIN		28.8g	29.8g	30.0g
CARBOHYDRATES		41.1g	41.1g	41.1g
SODIUM		1169mg	1166mg	1175mg
KILOJOULES		1357 (cal 324)	1325 (cal 316)	1325 (cal 316)

Sauces for Pasta

MEDITTERANEAN SAUCE

SERVES: 4

1 x 415g can diced tomatoes
1/4 cup sliced Spanish olives
1/3 cup sundried tomatoes sliced
1 cup onion diced
1 teaspoon crushed garlic (in jar)
1 teaspoon dried basil
1 teaspoon vegetable stock powder
1 cup evaporated light milk
1 tablespoon corn flour
cooking spray

> *Dietitions Tip* *A scrumptious sauce to serve with pasta.*
> *Pasta is a great basis to meals as it is high in fibre and has a low GI.*

In a non-stick saucepan that has been coated with cooking spray sauté onion and garlic for 2 minutes. Combine milk with cornflour, leave to one side. Add all other remaining ingredients except milk and bring to boil. Add in milk, return to boil then serve over pasta.

NUTRITIONAL INFORMATION:

PER SERVE		
FAT	TOTAL	4.5g
	SATURATED	1.1g
FIBRE		1.8g
PROTEIN		7.5g
CARBOHYDRATES		18.0g
SODIUM		404mg
KILOJOULES		600 (cal 143)

PESTO PASTA SAUCE

SERVES: 4

100ml (just over 1/3 cup) pesto paste (recipe below)
1 cup evaporated light milk
6 cups cooked fettuccini pasta

Prepare recipe below for PESTO PASTE. Place 1/3 of a cup of pesto paste in a large saucepan, combine with evaporated light milk. Once heated toss through 6 cups cooked fettuccini, serve when pasta is hot.

NUTRITIONAL INFORMATION

PER SERVE		
FAT	TOTAL	7.4g
	SATURATED	2.6g
FIBRE		5.2g
PROTEIN		18.2g
CARBOHYDRATES		64.2g
SODIUM		312mg
KILOJOULES		1681 (cal 401)

PESTO PASTE

MAKES: 2/3 cup or 24 teaspoons

1 bunch fresh basil (90g leaves only)
1 teaspoon crushed garlic (in jar)
1 tablespoon parmesan cheese
2 teaspoons virgin olive oil
1 heaped tablespoon pinenuts
1 teaspoon vegetable stock powder
1/4 cup water

Place pine nuts on a sheet of foil and brown under griller (be careful as they burn easily). Process pinenuts and garlic for 1 minute in a food processor. Add parmesan cheese, water, stock powder and basil leaves. Process for 2 minutes or until finely chopped. Add olive oil and process one minute. Refrigerate in a sealed jar.

> *Dietitions Tip*
> *Low fat Pesto Sauce – what a treat!*

NUTRITIONAL INFORMATION

PER SERVE		(1 TEASPOON)
FAT	TOTAL	0.8g
	SATURATED	0.2g
FIBRE		0.2g
PROTEIN		0.3g
CARBOHYDRATES		0.1g
SODIUM		37mg
KILOJOULES		39 (cal 9)

NUTRITIONAL INFORMATION ON PASTA ONLY

ALL PER 1 CUP COOKED PASTA

EGG PASTA		SPAGHETTI PASTA		FETTUCCINE PASTA	
FAT TOTAL	1.2g	FAT TOTAL	0.4g	FAT TOTAL	0.4g
SATURATED	0.2g	SATURATED	0g	SATURATED	0g
FIBRE	2.0g	FIBRE	2.7g	FIBRE	2.4g
PROTEIN	10.6g	PROTEIN	6.0g	PROTEIN	5.4g
CARBOHYDRATES	51.2g	CARBOHYDRATES	36.9g	CARBOHYDRATES	33.5g
SODIUM	6mg	SODIUM	3mg	SODIUM	3mg
KILOJOULES	1094 (cal 261)	KILOJOULES	745 (cal 178)	KILOJOULES	676 (cal 161)

BOSCAIOLA SAUCE

SERVES: 4

$^3/_4$ cup (85g) lean bacon short cut

1 cup onion finely diced

2 cups mushrooms sliced

1 cup capsicum diced

1 x 375ml can evaporated light milk

1 tablespoon tomato paste

1 teaspoon crushed garlic (in jar)

$^1/_8$ teaspoon chilli powder (or to taste)

2 teaspoons beef stock powder

1 tablespoon corn flour

salt and pepper to taste

Dice raw bacon and prepare vegetables as described. In a non-stick saucepan coated with cooking spray sauté bacon until browned. Add onion, capsicum and garlic, cook 2 minutes. Add mushrooms and cook 2 minutes. Add tomato paste, stock powder and chilli powder, combine corn flour with milk and add to pot, bring to boil. Salt and pepper to taste, serve over pasta.

NUTRITIONAL INFORMATION:

PER SERVE			PER SERVE	
FAT	TOTAL	3.0g	CARBOHYDRATES	16.8g
	SATURATED	2.0g	SODIUM	896mg
FIBRE		2.0g	KILOJOULES	655 (cal 156)
PROTEIN		15.0g		

SMOKED SALMON CREAM SAUCE

SERVES: 4

150g smoked salmon sliced

$^1/_3$ cup shallots sliced

1 teaspoon French mustard

$^1/_3$ cup white wine

1 tablespoon lemon juice

$^1/_2$ teaspoon dried dill

2 tablespoons tomato paste

$^3/_4$ cup skim milk

1 x 375ml can evaporated light milk

3 tablespoons corn flour

In a non-stick saucepan cook shallots, wine, mustard, lemon juice and dill, bring to boil, pour in evaporated milk. Add tomato paste and salmon and combine ingredients well. Mix corn flour and skim milk, add to pan, when boiled pour over pasta.

NUTRITIONAL INFORMATION:

PER SERVE			PER SERVE	
FAT	TOTAL	3.4g	CARBOHYDRATES	21.7g
	SATURATED	1.9g	SODIUM	840mg
FIBRE		0.5g	KILOJOULES	874 (cal 208)
PROTEIN		18.9g		

CREAMY PUMPKIN & PINENUT SAUCE

SERVES: 4

4 cups (580g) raw pumpkin diced
2 1/2 tablespoons pinenuts
1/2 cup onion finely diced
1 x 375ml can evaporated light milk
1 tablespoon tomato paste
1 teaspoon dried turmeric
1 teaspoon dried cumin
1 teaspoon dried coriander
1 teaspoon crushed garlic (in jar)
2 teaspoons vegetable or chicken stock powder
cooking spray
salt and pepper to taste

Roast pinenuts on a sheet of foil placed under the griller. In a little water microwave the diced pumpkin for about 6-7 minutes or until just cooked. Coat a non-stick saucepan with cooking spray and sauté onion and garlic for 2 minutes. Add turmeric, tomato paste, cumin, coriander and stock powder and cook 1 minute. Stir in evaporated milk and combine well. Add in drained cooked pumpkin, bring to boil and serve over pasta. Sprinkle pinenuts over each serve.

VARIATIONS:
Add 400g raw skinless CHICKEN BREAST diced when sautéing onion and garlic until chicken is cooked. Follow remainder of recipe as above or OMIT PINENUTS to reduce the fat count by 3.5g per serve.

NUTRITIONAL INFORMATION:		
PER SERVE	PUMPKIN	CHICKEN
FAT TOTAL	5.8g	8.1g
SATURATED	2.1g	2.7g
FIBRE	2.3g	2.3g
PROTEIN	11.7g	34.3g
CARBOHYDRATES	21.1g	21.1g
SODIUM	348mg	403mg
KILOJOULES	764 (cal 182)	1239 (cal 294)

TUSCANY SAUCE

SERVES: 4

1 x 410g can tomato puree
1 x 425g can crushed tomatoes
2 tablespoons tomato paste
1 teaspoon crushed garlic (in jar)
1 teaspoon dried basil
2 teaspoons beef stock powder
1 onion diced
1 cup capsicum diced
1 cup celery diced
1 cup zucchini diced
1 cup mushrooms sliced
salt & pepper to taste

In a large saucepan coated with cooking spray sauté garlic and vegetables for 3 minutes, stirring frequently. Add all other ingredients and simmer 10 minutes, stir occasionally. Salt and pepper to taste. Serve over pasta.

VARIATIONS:
Add 500g skinless CHICKEN BREAST cut into strips or add 500g lean BEEF strips or add 400g TOFU cubed

NUTRITIONAL INFORMATION:				
PER SERVE	TUSCANY	CHICKEN	BEEF	TOFU
FAT TOTAL	0.9g	3.7g	5.5g	6.9g
SATURATED	0.1g	0.9g	2.1g	0.1g
FIBRE	6.0g	6.0g	6.0g	6.0g
PROTEIN	5.0g	33.2g	32.0g	14.9g
CARBOHYDRATES	13.7g	13.7g	13.7g	17.7g
SODIUM	968mg	1037mg	1041mg	974mg
KILOJOULES	353 (cal 84)	939 (cal 224)	980 (cal 234)	707 (cal 169)

Desserts

MUD CAKE

SERVES: 12

28 squares (125g) good quality cooking chocolate
$^1/_2$ cup reduced fat margarine (Flora® light)
1 cup water
1 cup sugar
2 teaspoons instant coffee
2 egg whites
$^1/_2$ cup apple sauce (in jar)
$^1/_2$ teaspoon bi-carb soda
1$^1/_2$ cups plain flour
$^1/_4$ cup cocoa
cooking spray

ICING
1 cup icing sugar
1$^1/_2$ teaspoons reduced fat margarine (Flora® light)
2 level tablespoons cocoa
about 1 tablespoon skim milk

Preheat oven to 180°C fan forced.

Place chocolate, margarine, sugar, coffee and water into a ceramic bowl. Microwave on medium - low for 2 minutes, stir ingredients then return to microwave for another minute. Stir until all ingredients are dissolved. Stir bi-carb soda into apple sauce (it will froth) then add to bowl.

Add egg whites and mix well. Sift all the flour and cocoa into bowl then gently fold ingredients until combined. Pour mixture into a 19cm (8") round cake tin coated with cooking spray and bake 45-50 minutes or until cake springs back when lightly pressed in centre. When cool make icing.

ICING: In a small bowl sieve cocoa and icing sugar, add margarine and milk and mix until a smooth icing is made. Spread over cake. Refrigerate.

> *Dietitions Tip*   *Everyone's favourite! People with diabetes enjoy this one on special occasions.*

NUTRITIONAL INFORMATION:

PER SERVE		
FAT	TOTAL	9.0g
	SATURATED	3.1g
FIBRE		1.1g
PROTEIN		3.8g
CARBOHYDRATES		44.1g
SODIUM		67mg
KILOJOULES		1120 (cal 267)

* Mud cakes tend to crack a little on top.

SYMPLE SWEET CREAM

SERVES: 10

1 x 500g tub low fat cottage cheese
$^1/_2$ teaspoon vanilla essence
$^1/_3$ cup white sugar

In a food processor beat cottage cheese until very smooth. Add sugar and essence, beat until sugar has dissolved. Keep refrigerated.

> *Dietitions Tip*   *Well done Annette! This cream is deliciously low in fat and so versatile everyone will love it!*

NUTRITIONAL INFORMATION

PER SERVE		
FAT	TOTAL	0.6g
	SATURATED	0.4g
FIBRE		0g
PROTEIN		8.8g
CARBOHYDRATES		6.7g
SODIUM		65mg
KILOJOULES		280 (cal 67)

CHOC FUDGE SAUCE

SERVES: 12

1 x 375ml can evaporated light milk

2 tablespoons cocoa

1 tablespoon corn flour

125g (just under 1 cup) milk choc melts

2 x 11.5g Jarrah® Choc O'Lait sachets

In a medium size saucepan whisk together milk, cocoa, corn flour and Jarrah® Choc O'Lait until combined, cook on medium-high stirring continuously until just boiling. Remove from stove, add choc melts, mix together until chocolate has melted. Allow 2 tablespoons per serve.

VARIATION:
For a darker chocolate sauce replace milk choc melts with DARK CHOC MELTS.

Dietitions Tip Yum, this sauce is perfect over low fat ice cream or poured over fruit salad. Enjoy this in moderation.

NUTRITIONAL INFORMATION

PER SERVE			PER SERVE	
FAT	TOTAL	3.7g	CARBOHYDRATES	12.2g
	SATURATED	2.5g	SODIUM	66mg
FIBRE		0.1g	KILOJOULES	407 (cal 97)
PROTEIN		4.0g		

APPLE CRUMBLE

SERVES: 8

1 x 800g can pie apple (unsweetened)

1 cup self raising flour

2 Weetbix®

1/2 cup brown sugar

3 tablespoons reduced fat margarine (Flora® light)

1/2 teaspoon cinnamon

2 tablespoons skim milk

Preheat oven to 180°C fan forced. Melt margarine. In a medium size mixing bowl crush weetbix finely, add all other dry ingredients to bowl and combine. Add melted margarine into milk and blend into dry ingredients until mixture resembles a crumble texture. Place pie apple in base of a casserole dish (8 cup capacity), sprinkle crumble mixture over apple and bake 40-45 minutes.

Dietitions Tip Apples have a low GI. This is a great dish for everyone including people with diabetes. Serve with low fat ice cream.

NUTRITIONAL INFORMATION

PER SERVE			PER SERVE	
FAT	TOTAL	3.1g	CARBOHYDRATES	34.3g
	SATURATED	0.6g	SODIUM	172mg
FIBRE		2.0g	KILOJOULES	728 (cal 174)
PROTEIN		2.7g		

CHOCOLATE PUDDING

SERVES: 8

1 x 375ml can evaporated light milk

1 1/2 cups skim milk

2 x 10g gelatine sachets

1/4 cup boiling water

3/4 cup chocolate topping

2 x 11.5g Jarrah® Choc O'Lait sachets

1 teaspoon sifted cocoa

Heat both milks together in microwave 2 minutes. Using a whisk dissolve cocoa, Jarrah® sachets and chocolate topping into milk. Dissolve gelatine in boiled water and beat into milk. Leave to set in refrigerator.

NUTRITIONAL INFORMATION

PER SERVE			PER SERVE	
FAT	TOTAL	1.3g	CARBOHYDRATES	21.7g
	SATURATED	0.9g	SODIUM	128mg
FIBRE		0g	KILOJOULES	548 (cal 131)
PROTEIN		8.5g		

CRÉME CARAMELS

MAKES: 6

CUSTARD
3 whole eggs

3 egg whites

3 cups skim milk

$^1/_2$ teaspoon vanilla essence

$^1/_2$ cup castor sugar

CARAMEL TOFFEE
$^3/_4$ cup sugar

$^3/_4$ cup water

Preheat oven to 160°C fan forced.

You will require 6 ovenproof tea cups to make the crème caramels in.

In a non-stick saucepan make caramel toffee by bringing sugar and water to the boil, reduce heat slightly and continue on a slow boil for about 10-15 minutes (don't stir). Keep an eye on the toffee as it can burn quickly. Once the toffee is a nice golden brown colour remove from heat and pour equal amounts into each of the tea cups. Leave to one side. To make the custard beat eggs in a large mixing bowl until blended. Add in all other ingredients and beat until well combined. Pour equal amounts of custard into the 6 tea cups. Place in a large baking pan that has been half filled with water. Bake for 40-50 minutes depending on size of cup or until custard is firm to touch. Leave to cool. To remove from cups run a sharp knife around the edge of cup, turn over onto a dessert plate and whilst holding the plate and cup together shake down to release créme caramel.

Dietitions Tip This is a great alternative to traditional créme caramel, people with diabetes enjoy this one on special occasions!

CARAMEL BANANA SELF SAUCING PUDDING

SERVES: 8

1$^1/_2$ cups self raising flour

$^3/_4$ cup mashed banana (2 medium bananas)

$^1/_3$ cup brown sugar

2 egg whites

$^1/_2$ cup apple sauce (in jar)

$^3/_4$ teaspoon bi-carb soda

1 cup brown sugar

1$^1/_2$ cups water

Pre heat oven to 180°C fan forced.

In a medium size mixing bowl beat egg whites and sugar for 1 minute using an electric beater. Stir bi-carb into apple sauce (it will froth) then add to bowl. Add mashed bananas and combine. Gently fold flour into mixture in one go, DO NOT BEAT as this will make the pudding tough. Pour pudding mixture into a casserole dish (8 cup capacity).

To make caramel sauce sprinkle 1 cup of brown sugar over top of pudding mixture, gently pour water over the top. Bake 30-35 minutes or until firm to touch in centre.

Dietitions Tip Everyone loves pudding, people with diabetes can enjoy this one but go for a smaller serve.

NUTRITIONAL INFORMATION:

PER SERVE		
FAT	TOTAL	0.3g
	SATURATED	0.1g
FIBRE		1.5g
PROTEIN		3.8g
CARBOHYDRATES		48.6g
SODIUM		203mg
KILOJOULES		875(cal 209)

NUTRITIONAL INFORMATION:

PER SERVE			PER SERVE	
FAT	TOTAL	2.6g	CARBOHYDRATES	43.0g
	SATURATED	1.0g	SODIUM	116mg
FIBRE		0g	KILOJOULES	944 (cal 225)
PROTEIN		9.5g		

BAKED CHEESECAKE

SERVES: 12

BASE
15 arrowroot biscuits

3 tablespoons skim milk

cooking spray

FILLING
125g light Philadelphia® reduced fat cream cheese

500g tub low fat cottage cheese

1 tablespoon lemon rind

3 tablespoons lemon juice

3/4 cup sugar

1 teaspoon vanilla essence

3 tablespoons plain flour

2 egg whites

1 whole egg

BERRY SAUCE
1 x 425g can mixed berries

1 tablespoon corn flour

Preheat oven to 160°C fan forced.

BASE: In a food processor crumble biscuits, add milk and blend together. Coat a 22cm spring based cake tin with cooking spray and press biscuit mix into base using the palm of your hand. Refrigerate whilst making the filling.

FILLING: Clean food processor bowl and add cottage cheese, blend until very smooth, add cream cheese and blend. Put in rind, lemon juice and essence, blend ingredients. Slowly add in sugar until dissolved. Add eggs and combine with mixture, finally add flour. Pour mixture over biscuit base. Bake for 1 hour. Once removed from oven gently release edge of tin to loosen cake away from edge, this may help stop cracking as it cools.

BERRY SAUCE: Place both ingredients into a small saucepan and bring to boil, stirring continuously. Leave to cool. Pour sauce over each slice of cheesecake.

> *Dietitions Tip* *This one's a winner.*
> *Everyone will love this low fat cheesecake!*

NUTRITIONAL INFORMATION:

PER SERVE		C/CAKE with sauce	C/CAKE plain
FAT	TOTAL	4.3g	4.3g
	SATURATED	0.5g	0.5g
FIBRE		1.0g	0.4g
PROTEIN		10.6g	10.5g
CARBOHYDRATES		29.5g	22.7g
SODIUM		136mg	135mg
KILOJOULES		829 (cal 198)	714 (cal 170)

CUSTARD TART

SERVES: 10

PASTRY
$^1/_4$ cup self raising flour
$^3/_4$ cup plain flour
3 tablespoons reduced fat margarine (Flora® light)
2 tablespoons sugar
1 egg white
1 tablespoon skim milk
cooking spray

CUSTARD FILLING
2 whole eggs
3 egg whites
3 cups skim milk
1 teaspoon vanilla essence
$^1/_4$ cup sugar
nutmeg

Preheat oven to 180°C fan forced.

PASTRY: In a large mixing bowl combine flours and sugar. Melt margarine and add to milk. Using a fork mix egg white into milk mixture until combined, pour into flour mixture and knead together with your hands. On a floured surface roll out pastry to fit a 23 cm pie dish that has been coated with cooking spray.

CUSTARD: In a large mixing bowl beat eggs, milk, essence and sugar together well. Slide oven rack out and place pie dish in centre, pour custard filling into pie dish and sprinkle top generously with nutmeg. Very gently slide rack back into oven. Bake tart for 45-50 minutes or until custard is firm to touch.

NUTRITIONAL INFORMATION:					
PER SERVE			PER SERVE		
FAT	TOTAL	3.4g	CARBOHYDRATES		21.4g
	SATURATED	0.8g	SODIUM		111mg
FIBRE		0.5g	KILOJOULES	598 (cal 143)	
PROTEIN		6.9g			

MANGO MOUSSE

SERVES: 8

2 x 450g cans sliced mango drained (Golden Circle®)
250g tub low fat cottage cheese
1 cup CHILLED evaporated light milk
$^1/_2$ cup sugar
1 x 10g gelatine sachet
$^1/_4$ cup boiling water

You will need to have a can of evaporated milk chilled overnight for this recipe.

In a food processor blend cottage cheese until very smooth, add mango and process until combined, slowly add sugar and blend until dissolved. In a large mixing bowl beat evaporated milk with an electric beater until thick and stiff (about 5 minutes). Beat the mango mixture into the milk until blended. In a $^1/_4$ cup of boiled water add gelatine, stir until dissolved. Add this to the mango mixture and beat until all ingredients are well combined. Leave to set in refrigerator.

VARIATION:
Replace canned mango with any CANNED FRUIT of your choice.

> *Dietitians Tip* A cool summer dessert incorporating everyone's favourite – mangoes!

NUTRITIONAL INFORMATION:		
PER SERVE		
FAT	TOTAL	1.0g
	SATURATED	0.8g
FIBRE		0.7g
PROTEIN		9.7g
CARBOHYDRATES		31.0g
SODIUM		75mg
KILOJOULES		704 (cal 168)

RASPBERRY CHEESECAKE

SERVES: 12

BASE
15 arrowroot biscuits

1 tablespoon reduced fat margarine (Flora® light)

3 tablespoons skim milk

cooking spray

FILLING
1 x 300g pkt frozen raspberries

500g low fat cottage cheese

125g Light Philadelphia® reduced fat cream cheese

1 teaspoon vanilla essence

$^1/_2$ cup sugar

1 x 9g pkt raspberry low joule jelly crystals

1 teaspoon gelatine

$^1/_3$ cup boiled water

FRUIT TOPPING
raspberries remaining from filling

$^1/_2$ cup water

$^1/_4$ cup sugar

2 teaspoons gelatine

BASE: Melt margarine. In a food processor crumble biscuits, add milk and margarine and blend together. Coat a 22cm spring based cake tin with cooking spray, press biscuit mix into base using the palm of your hand. Refrigerate.

FILLING: Clean food processor bowl and add cottage cheese, blend until very smooth. Add cream cheese and blend. Slowly pour sugar in and mix until dissolved. Add essence and 1 cup of frozen raspberries, blend well (leave remaining raspberries for topping). Combine jelly and gelatine in boiled water until dissolved, pour into blender, once ingredients are thoroughly mixed pour over biscuit base and refrigerate until set.

TOPPING: In a small saucepan combine the remaining raspberries, water, sugar and gelatine. Just bring to boil and leave to cool slightly. Gently pour over cheesecake, refrigerate until set.

NUTRITIONAL INFORMATION:		
PER SERVE		
FAT	TOTAL	4.6g
	SATURATED	0.5g
FIBRE		2.5g
PROTEIN		11.2g
CARBOHYDRATES		23.0g
SODIUM		132mg
KILOJOULES		747 (cal 178)

TIRAMISYM

SERVES: 12

SPONGE

¹/₂ cup corn flour

¹/₄ cup self raising flour

2 tablespoons custard powder

2 whole eggs

2 egg whites

¹/₂ cup caster sugar

³/₄ teaspoon bi-carb soda

1 teaspoon baking powder

cooking spray

Preheat oven to 180°C fan forced.

In a large mixing bowl beat egg whites with an electric beater until stiff peaks form. Gradually add in sugar beating constantly. Beat in egg yolks on low speed. Using a large spoon, gently fold in the sifted corn flour, self raising flour, custard powder, bi-carb soda and baking powder. Pour mixture into a lamington tin (31cm x 25cm) that has been coated with cooking spray and bake 15-20 minutes until centre springs back when touched. Allow sponge to sit 5 minutes in tray before turning onto a wire rack to cool.

COFFEE SYRUP

1 cup boiling water

3 teaspoons instant coffee

¹/₃ cup sugar

¹/₄ cup Tia Maria® liqueur

Combine ingredients and leave to one side to cool.

CREAM FILLING

1 x 500g tub low fat cottage cheese

¹/₂ teaspoon vanilla essence

¹/₃ cup white sugar

In a food processor beat cottage cheese until really smooth. Add sugar and essence and beat until sugar has dissolved. Keep refrigerated until required.

TO ASSEMBLE TIRAMISYM

Cut sponge in half to make two pieces. Cut through each piece widthways so you have 4 layers of sponge. Place first layer onto plate for serving. Spoon a quarter of the coffee syrup evenly over sponge, top with a third of the cream spreading evenly. Top with a layer of sponge with the cut side facing up and repeat coffee syrup and cream. Repeat again. On final layer of sponge place cut side facing down, spoon coffee mixture over top. Sprinkle a little cocoa and icing sugar over top for decoration. Refrigerate until required.

NUTRITIONAL INFORMATION:		
PER SERVE		
FAT	TOTAL	1.4g
	SATURATED	0.6g
FIBRE		0.3g
PROTEIN		9.4g
CARBOHYDRATES		31.7g
SODIUM		95mg
KILOJOULES		767 (cal 183)

Baking

LIGHT SPONGE

SERVES: 8

¹/₂ cup corn flour

¹/₄ cup self raising flour

2 tablespoons custard powder

2 whole eggs

2 egg whites

¹/₂ cup caster sugar

³/₄ teaspoon bi-carb soda

1 teaspoon baking powder

cooking spray

Preheat oven to 180°C fan forced.

In a large mixing bowl beat egg whites with an electric beater until stiff peaks form. Gradually add sugar beating constantly. Beat in egg yolks on low speed. Using a large spoon, gently fold in the sifted corn flour, self raising flour, bi-carb soda, baking powder and custard powder. Divide mixture between two sponge tins (about 18cm) that have been coated with cooking spray and bake 15-20 minutes until centre springs back when touched. Allow sponge to sit 5 minutes in tray before turning onto a wire rack to cool.

VARIATION:
JAM & CREAM SPONGE- Spread ¹/₄ cup berry jam over top of one sponge. Make a half batch of SYMPLE SWEET CREAM on page 51 and spread over top of jam, place other sponge on top and sprinkle top with a little icing sugar. Keep refrigerated.

NUTRITIONAL INFORMATION:

PER SERVE		PLAIN	JAM/CREAM SPONGE
FAT	TOTAL	1.3g	1.7g
	SATURATED	0.4g	0.6g
FIBRE		0.2g	0.3g
PROTEIN		2.8g	8.4g
CARBOHYDRATES		26.7g	39.0g
SODIUM		61mg	103mg
KILOJOULES		536 (cal 128)	843 (cal 201)

LIGHT TROPICAL FRUIT CAKE

SERVES: 10

2 cups self raising flour

1 x 375g pkt dried fruit medley

1 x 450g can sliced mango drained (Golden Circle®)

1 teaspoon bi-carb soda

¹/₃ cup sugar

3 egg whites

1 teaspoon cinnamon

1 teaspoon mixed spice

1 cup water

cooking spray

In a medium size saucepan place fruit medley, sugar, spices, water and mango, bring to boil and boil for 3 minutes. Stir in bi-carb soda, leave to cool.

Preheat oven to 180°C fan forced. When fruit mixture has cooled beat egg whites into fruit. Fold in flour. Pour mixture into a 19cm (8") round tin or large loaf tin that has been coated with cooking spray and bake approximately 40-45 minutes or until firm to touch in centre. Allow cake to sit for 5 minutes in tin before turning onto a wire rack to cool.

In humid weather this cake is best kept refrigerated.

Dietitions Tip Fruit is a great GI food to base cakes on. This cake is packed with carbohydrates so people with diabetes should have a small slice.

NUTRITIONAL INFORMATION:

PER SERVE		
FAT	TOTAL	0.7g
	SATURATED	0.1g
FIBRE		0.5g
PROTEIN		5.0g
CARBOHYDRATES		58.4g
SODIUM		211mg
KILOJOULES		1040 (cal 248)

ALMOND APRICOT BREAD

SERVES: 10

1 cup plain flour
$^1/_2$ cup caster sugar
3 egg whites
$^1/_2$ cup whole raw almonds
$^1/_2$ cup dried apricots (cut in half)
cooking spray

Preheat oven to 160°C fan forced.

In a medium size mixing bowl beat egg whites for 1 minute. Gradually add sugar and beat 2 more minutes. Add almonds and apricots and fold together with a large spoon. In one go add flour and gently fold through. Pour into a loaf tin (about 9 x 20cm) that has been coated with cooking spray and bake for 30-40 minutes or when firm to touch in centre. Allow loaf to sit 5 minutes in tin before turning onto a wire rack to cool. When cooled wrap in plastic wrap and place in refrigerator for 24 hours.

NEXT DAY: Preheat oven to 160°C fan forced. Using a sharp knife cut loaf into 50 very thin slices. Place each slice on a flat baking tray and bake until dry, about 10 minutes.

Dietitions tips
This recipe contains a great balance of healthy fats.

NUTRITIONAL INFORMATION:		
PER SERVE		(5 SLICES PER SERVE)
FAT	TOTAL	4.2g
	SATURATED	0.3g
FIBRE		1.8g
PROTEIN		4.3g
CARBOHYDRATES		22.7g
SODIUM		20mg
KILOJOULES		604 (cal 144)

PASSIONFRUIT CAKE

SERVES: 10

2 cups self raising flour
1 teaspoon bi-carb soda
3 egg whites
$^3/_4$ cup sugar
4 tablespoons reduced fat margarine melted (Flora® light)
$^1/_2$ cup passionfruit pulp (about 4)
1 cup water
cooking spray

ICING
$^3/_4$ cup icing sugar
1 tablespoon passionfruit pulp (about 1)
1 teaspoon reduced fat margarine (Flora® light)

Preheat oven to 180°C fan forced.

In a large mixing bowl beat egg whites and sugar together for 1 minute. Add passionfruit pulp, water, melted margarine and combine well. In one go gently fold in sifted flour and bi-carb, DO NOT BEAT as this will make the cake tough. Pour into a 19 cm cake tin and bake for 35-40 minutes or until firm to touch in centre. Allow cake to sit 5 minutes in tin before turning onto a wire rack to cool.

ICING: Once cake has cooled place all icing ingredients in a small mixing bowl, blend together until smooth. Spread over top of cake.

VARIATIONS:
To make a VANILLA CAKE omit passionfruit pulp and add ¼ cup more water to cake mix. For icing add milk instead of passionfruit pulp
or to make an ORANGE CAKE omit passionfruit pulp, and replace 1 cup water with 1¼ cup orange juice unsweetened and 3 small tablespoons grated orange rind. Use orange juice for icing instead of passionfruit pulp.

NUTRITIONAL INFORMATION:				
PER SERVE			PER SERVE	
FAT	TOTAL	3.6 g	CARBOHYDRATES	44.8g
	SATURATED	0.7g	SODIUM	243mg
FIBRE		5.5g	KILOJOULES	967 (cal 231)
PROTEIN		4.8g		

ROCK CAKES

MAKES: 12

2 cups self raising flour

$^1/_4$ cup sugar

4 tablespoons reduced fat margarine (Flora® light)

1 cup dried mixed fruit

$^1/_4$ teaspoon cinnamon

$^1/_2$ cup skim milk

2 egg whites

2 teaspoons sugar to sprinkle on top

Preheat oven to 200°C fan forced.

Place all dry ingredients except extra sugar into a large mixing bowl. Melt margarine and add to milk, combine. Add egg whites to milk mix, using a fork beat together until combined. Add milk mixture to dry ingredients and mix well.

On a flat baking tray coated with cooking spray place large spoonfuls of mixture, making 12. Sprinkle extra sugar on top of each one, bake 20 minutes.

Dietitions tips
These rock cakes are a perfect between meal snack.

TOOTY FRUITY SQUARES

MAKES: 15 squares

BASE

2 cups self raising flour

1 x 440g can traditional fruit salad (in natural juice)

2 egg whites

$^1/_2$ cup sugar

$^1/_2$ cup apple sauce (in jar)

$^3/_4$ teaspoon bi-carb soda

cooking spray

ICING

1 cup icing sugar

1 teaspoon reduced fat margarine (Flora® light)

about 1 tablespoon saved fruit salad juice

Preheat oven to 180°C fan forced.

Drain fruit salad, saving the juice for icing. In a medium size mixing bowl beat egg whites and sugar for 1 minute using an electric beater. Stir bi-carb into apple sauce (it will froth) then add to bowl. Add drained fruit salad and combine all ingredients. Gently fold flour into mixture in one go, DO NOT BEAT as this will make the cake tough. Pour mixture into a slab tin coated with cooking spray. Bake 25 minutes or until firm to touch in centre.

ICING: Once slice has cooled place all icing ingredients into a small mixing bowl, combine well. Spread evenly over top of slice. Once set cut into 15 squares.

NUTRITIONAL INFORMATION:

PER ROCK CAKE

FAT	TOTAL	2.9g
	SATURATED	0.6g
FIBRE		1.5g
PROTEIN		3.5g
CARBOHYDRATES		28.8g
SODIUM		204mg
KILOJOULES		645 (cal 154)

NUTRITIONAL INFORMATION:

PER SERVE

FAT	TOTAL	0.4g
	SATURATED	0.1g
FIBRE		1.1g
PROTEIN		2.5g
CARBOHYDRATES		29.9g
SODIUM		139mg
KILOJOULES		550 (cal 131)

JAM CRUMBLE SLICE

MAKES: 15 Slices

2 cups self raising flour

1/2 cup brown sugar

6 tablespoons reduced fat margarine (Flora® light)

1 cup raw rolled oats

1/4 cup skim milk

3/4 cup jam

cooking spray

Preheat oven to 180°C fan forced.

In a large mixing bowl combine all dry ingredients. Melt margarine, mix together with milk and add to dry mix. Mix all ingredients together well. In a slab tin coated with cooking spray place a little more than half the mixture over the base, pressing down with the palm of your hand. Warm jam slightly in microwave then spread evenly over base. Sprinkle remaining dough over jam then press down with your hand or the back of a large spoon until mixture is flattened. Bake 30-35 minutes or until golden brown on top. When cool cut into slices.

Dietitions Tip Rolled oats have low GI.
This is a great snack for people with diabetes.

NUTRITIONAL INFORMATION:

PER SERVE

FAT	TOTAL	3.4g
	SATURATED	0.7g
FIBRE		1.1g
PROTEIN		2.5g
CARBOHYDRATES		30.1g
SODIUM		160gm
KILOJOULES		674 (cal 161)

MUESLI FRUIT SLICE

MAKES: 15 Slices

2 cups low fat muesli (Sanitarium®)

1 cup self raising flour

1/3 cup brown sugar

1/3 cup honey

6 tablespoons reduced fat margarine (Flora® light)

1 egg white

1/2 cup dried fruit medley

cooking spray

Preheat oven to 180°C fan forced.

In microwave melt margarine with honey. In a large mixing bowl combine all dry ingredients. Add margarine mixture and egg white to dry ingredients, combine well. Press into slab tin coated with cooking spray. Bake 20-25 minutes or until golden brown. When cool cut into 15 slices.

Dietitions Tip This slice is an excellent snack
for people with diabetes.

NUTRITIONAL INFORMATION:

PER SERVE

FAT	TOTAL	3.4g
	SATURATED	0.6g
FIBRE		1.5g
PROTEIN		2.3g
CARBOHYDRATES		28.7g
SODIUM		125mg
KILOJOULES		641 (cal 153)

HUMMINGBIRD CAKE

SERVES: 12

2 cups self raising flour

2 egg whites

$^1/_3$ cup sugar

$^1/_2$ cup apple sauce (in jar)

1 teaspoon bi-carb soda

$^3/_4$ cup drained canned crushed pineapple
(in natural juice)

1 cup mashed banana

$^1/_4$ cup (25g) walnuts chopped

1 teaspoon mixed spice

cooking spray

ICING

1 cup icing sugar

about 1 tablespoon saved pineapple juice (from can)

2 teaspoons reduced fat margarine (Flora® light)

Preheat oven to 180°C fan forced.

Drain pineapple keeping juice for icing. In a large mixing bowl beat egg whites and sugar for 1 minute using an electric beater. Stir bi-carb into apple sauce (it will froth) and add to bowl. Mix in mashed banana, walnuts, drained pineapple and mixed spice, blend ingredients together well. Gently fold flour into mixture in one go, DO NOT BEAT, as this will make the cake tough. Pour mixture into a round cake tin (19cm) that has been coated with cooking spray. Bake 35-40 minutes or until firm to touch in centre. Allow cake to sit for 5 minutes in tin before turning onto a wire rack to cool.

ICING: Once cake has cooled place all icing ingredients into a small mixing bowl, blend together until smooth. Spread over top of cake. In humid weather it is best to keep this cake refrigerated.

Dietitions Tip   Annette, you have done it again! This is a fantastic low fat alternative to the traditional Hummingbird cake! Everyone can enjoy a slice of this cake!

NUTRITIONAL INFORMATION		
PER SERVE		
FAT	TOTAL	2.0g
	SATURATED	0.2g
FIBRE		1.8g
PROTEIN		3.6g
CARBOHYDRATES		38.1g
SODIUM		175mg
KILOJOULES		763 (cal 182)

IMPORTANT BAKING TIP

When baking cakes please follow these few tips to make the best cakes ever – because there are hardly any fats in these recipes there is nothing to protect the gluten so every time you move the flour you bruise it. That is why you need to add all the flour in one go, and you shouldn't beat but gently fold it through. If too heavy handed your cakes may come out tough, this tells you that you are moving the flour too much. I am sure you will enjoy this delicious baking section if you just follow this advice.

SAVOURY SCONE SCROLLS

MAKES: 12 Scrolls

SCONE DOUGH

2¼ cups self raising flour

2 tablespoons reduced fat margarine (Flora® light)

1 egg white

¾ cup skim milk

pinch salt

cooking spray

extra skim milk for brushing

extra flour for rolling dough

FILLING

½ cup grated 25% reduced fat tasty cheese

2 tablespoons parmesan cheese

½ cup shallots sliced

½ cup capsicum diced

1 cup lean ham diced

Preheat oven to 220°C fan forced.

Place flour and salt in a large mixing bowl. Melt margarine and add to milk. Using a fork beat egg white into milk until combined, pour into flour and fold together. Place dough on a well floured surface and roll out into an oblong shape 32 x 24cm in size. With the widest side nearest yourself brush with a little extra milk. In a small bowl combine all of the filling ingredients together. Sprinkle evenly over dough. Starting from the widest side roll dough away from yourself ending with the edge underneath to form a tight roll. Cut roll in half then half again, cut each piece into 3 slices, making 12 slices all up. On a flat baking tray coated with cooking spray, place scones flat side down touching each other in a round cluster. Brush with a little milk and bake 12-15 minutes.

NUTRITIONAL INFORMATION:

PER SCROLL			PER SCROLL	
FAT	TOTAL	3.3g	CARBOHYDRATES	19.7g
	SATURATED	1.4g	SODIUM	304mg
FIBRE		1.0g	KILOJOULES	561 (cal 134)
PROTEIN		6.0g		

FRUIT SCONE SCROLLS

MAKES: 12 Scrolls

SCONE DOUGH

2¼ cups self raising flour

2 tablespoons reduced fat margarine (Flora® light)

1 tablespoon sugar

1 egg white

¾ cup skim milk

cooking spray

extra skim milk for brushing

extra flour for rolling dough

FILLING

¼ cup sugar

1 teaspoon cinnamon

½ cup sultanas

Preheat oven to 220°C fan forced.

Place flour and sugar in a large mixing bowl. Melt margarine and add to milk. Using a fork beat egg white into milk until combined, pour into flour and fold together. Place dough onto a well floured surface and roll out into an oblong shape 32 x 24cm in size. With the widest side nearest yourself brush with a little extra milk. Combine sugar and cinnamon together, sprinkle evenly over dough, sprinkle sultanas over top. Starting from the widest side roll dough away from yourself ending with the edge underneath to form a tight roll. Cut roll in half then half again, cut each piece into 3 slices, making 12 slices all up. On a flat baking tray coated with cooking spray, place scones flat side down touching each other in a round cluster. Brush with a little milk and bake 12-15 minutes.

NUTRITIONAL INFORMATION:

PER SCROLL			PER SCROLL	
FAT	TOTAL	1.6g	CARBOHYDRATES	30.3g
	SATURATED	0.3g	SODIUM	208mg
FIBRE		1.3g	KILOJOULES	630 (cal 151)
PROTEIN		3.8g		

STICKY LEMON LOAF

SERVES: 10

1 1/2 cups self raising flour
2 egg whites
1/2 cup sugar
2 tablespoons reduced fat margarine (Flora® light)
3/4 cup skim milk
3/4 teaspoon bi-carb soda
2 tablespoons lemon juice
2 tablespoons lemon rind
cooking spray

SYRUP
3/4 cup lemon juice
1/4 cup icing sugar

Preheat oven to 180°C fan forced.

In a large mixing bowl beat egg whites and sugar for 1 minute. Add lemon rind, lemon juice, melted margarine and milk, mix together well. In one go gently fold in flour and bi-carb to mixture, DO NOT BEAT as this will make the loaf tough. Pour into a loaf tin (21 x 10cm) that has been coated with cooking spray. Bake 30 minutes or until firm to touch in centre.

SYRUP: To make syrup combine juice and icing sugar together. When cake is cooked prick a few holes in the top with a fork, pour syrup over cake, leave to sit for 2 minutes then remove loaf from tin and turn onto wire rack to cool.

VARIATIONS: *Replace lemon juice and rind with orange juice and rind for a STICKY ORANGE LOAF or, replace lemon juice and rind with 1/2 lemon and 1/2 orange juice and rind for a STICKY CITRUS LOAF*

NUTRITIONAL INFORMATION:

PER SERVE			PER SERVE	
FAT	TOTAL	1.8g	CARBOHYDRATES	28.2g
	SATURATED	0.4g	SODIUM	177mg
FIBRE		0.8g	KILOJOULES.	600 (cal 143)
PROTEIN		3.5g		

GOLDEN OAT CRUNCHES

MAKES: 24 Cookies

1 cup plain flour
1 cup raw rolled oats
1/2 cup brown sugar
1 teaspoon bi-carb soda
5 tablespoons reduced fat margarine (Flora® light)
2 tablespoons golden syrup
cooking spray

Preheat oven to 150°C fan forced.

In a large mixing bowl combine all dry ingredients. Melt margarine, mix together with golden syrup then add to dry mix. Combine ingredients together well. Coat a large baking tray with cooking spray, roll about 1 teaspoon of mixture into a ball then place on tray, flatten with the back of a fork, repeat until you have 24 cookies. Allow space for biscuits to spread a little. Bake 20 minutes, leave to cool on tray.

Dietitions Tip Oats are great for people with diabetes as they have low GI. A great snack idea Annette!

NUTRITIONAL INFORMATION:

PER COOKIE		
FAT	TOTAL	2.0g
	SATURATED	0.4g
FIBRE		0.5g
PROTEIN		1.0g
CARBOHYDRATES		12.0g
SODIUM		16mg
KILOJOULES		288 (cal 68)

CARAMEL TARTS

MAKES: 24 Tarts

PASTRY
3/4 cup plain flour
1/4 cup self raising flour
1 egg white
2 tablespoons sugar
2 tablespoons reduced fat margarine (Flora® light)
1 tablespoon skim milk
extra flour to roll pastry
cooking spray

FILLING
1 cup evaporated light milk
1 x 400g can condensed light milk
1/4 cup brown sugar
2 tablespoons reduced fat margarine (Flora® light)
1 tablespoon corn flour
small amount of water

Preheat oven to 180°C fan forced.

PASTRY: Place flour and sugar in a medium size mixing bowl. Melt margarine and add to milk. Using a fork beat egg white into milk until combined, pour into flour and fold together. Place pastry onto a well floured surface and roll thinly. Using a 7cm scone cutter cut out 24 pastry bases. Place 12 bases in a patty pan tin that has been coated with cooking spray. Bake 10 minutes or until lightly browned, remove and cool on a wire rack. Wash tray and repeat procedure with remaining 12 pastry bases.

FILLING: In a small mixing bowl whisk together evaporated milk and condensed milk, leave to one side. In a non-stick saucepan melt margarine, add in brown sugar and combine, once sugar has dissolved remove from heat and whisk in milk mixture. Place back on stove and bring to boil on a medium to high temperature (so as not to burn bottom of pot) you must stir continuously. Once boiled reduce to a slow boil until mixture is a caramel colour, about 15 minutes, stir frequently. In a small amount of water dissolve corn flour and stir in to pot. Once boiled remove from heat and allow to cool. Spoon filling into pastry cases.

> *Dietitians Tip*   Sheer indulgence, everyone can enjoy this delicious tart!

NUTRITIONAL INFORMATION:

PER TART		
TOTAL	FAT	1.5g
	SATURATED	0.5g
FIBRE		0.2g
PROTEIN		3.3g
CARBOHYDRATES		18.4g
SODIUM		54mg
KILOJOULES		413 (cals 98)

LIGHT MARS BAR SLICE

MAKES: 15 Slices

BASE
2 x 44.5g Mars Bars® lite 50% less fat
3 cups Rice Bubbles®
2 tablespoons golden syrup
1 tablespoon reduced fat margarine (Flora lite®)
1 tablespoon skim milk
cooking spray

ICING
3/4 cup icing sugar
2 tablespoons cocoa
1-2 tablespoons skim milk

BASE: Place Rice Bubbles in a large mixing bowl. In a microwave safe bowl place roughly chopped Mars Bars, margarine and golden syrup, melt on high for 2 minutes, stir well, return to microwave for a further 30 seconds. Add milk and stir mixture until smooth. Pour melted chocolate mixture into rice bubbles, stirring until covered with chocolate mix. Coat a slab tin with cooking spray and press mixture into tin evenly. Refrigerate.

ICING: Once slice is set place all icing ingredients into a small mixing bowl and mix together well. Spread icing over base and refrigerate. Once set cut into 15 slices.

This slice is best kept refrigerated.

VARIATIONS:
Replace lite Mars Bars with 2 x 55g TURKISH DELIGHT bars. Change base by using only 1 tablespoon golden syrup, then follow as per recipe above.
Mars® is a registered trademark ©2001.

Dietitions Tip This delicious slice will be popular *with everyone and is suitable for people with diabetes.*

NUTRITIONAL INFORMATION:			
PER SERVE		MARS	TURKISH
FAT	TOTAL	1.3g	1.3g
	SATURATED	0.2g	0.2g
FIBRE		0.1g	0.1g
PROTEIN		0.8g	0.8g
CARBOHYDRATES		18.8g	18.1g
SODIUM		89mg	81mg
KILOJOULES		363 (cal 87)	362 (cal 86)

Index

If you would like Annette to come and speak to your group, conference or seminar please phone/fax:

**The Symply Too Good To Be True Hotline (07) 5493 6750 (Int: +61 7 5493 6750)
Annette's Web Site: www.symplytoogood.com.au**

For information on stockists phone/fax the hotline or Email: symply@mpx.com.au

THREE EASY ORDER METHODS AVAILABLE	
1. Website – secure online credit card orders Australia and International
2. Hotline – for credit card orders Australia and International
3. Mail Order – send cheque/money order made payable to Annette Sym PO Box 833, Buddina, Qld 4575 (prices below) Australia only. Please specify clearly whether order is for 1st, 2nd or 3rd cookbook and quantities of each. (Allow 7-21 days for delivery - Don't forget to include your mailing address)

Quantity:

1 Book (incl. GST)	$11.95
Postage	$3.50
Total	$15.45

2 Books (incl. GST)	$23.90
Postage	$6.00
Total	$29.90

3-10 Books (incl. GST)	$11.95 ea. book
Postage	$8.00